THE LITTLE BOOK

of

COMMON SENSE
INVESTING

Little Book Big Profits Series

In the *Little Book Big Profits* series, the brightest icons in the financial world write on topics that range from tried-and-true investment strategies we've come to appreciate to tomorrow's new trends.

Books in the *Little Book Big Profits* series include:

The Little Book That Beats the Market, where Joel Greenblatt, founder and managing partner at Gotham Capital, reveals a "magic formula" that is easy to use and makes buying good companies at bargain prices automatic, giving you the opportunity to beat the market and professional managers by a wide margin.

The Little Book of Value Investing, where Christopher Browne, managing director of Tweedy, Browne Company, LLC, the oldest value investing firm on Wall Street, simply and succinctly explains how value investing, one of the most effective investment strategies ever created, works, and shows you how it can be applied globally.

The Little Book of Common Sense Investing, where Vanguard Group founder John C. Bogle shares his own time-tested philosophies, lessons, and personal anecdotes to explain why outperforming the market is an investor illusion, and how the simplest of investment strategies—indexing—can deliver the greatest return to the greatest number of investors.

THE LITTLE BOOK

of

COMMON SENSE

INVESTING

The Only Way to Guarantee Your
Fair Share of Stock Market Returns

JOHN C. BOGLE

BICENTENNIAL
1807
WILEY
2007
BICENTENNIAL

John Wiley & Sons, Inc.

Published by John Wiley & Sons, Inc., Hoboken, New Jersey.
Published simultaneously in Canada.

Wiley Bicentennial Logo: Richard J. Pacifico

For general information on our other products and services or for technical support, please contact our Customer Care Department within the United States at (800) 762-2974, outside the United States at (317) 572-3993 or fax (317) 572-4002.

Wiley also publishes its books in a variety of electronic formats. Some content that appears in print may not be available in electronic books. For more information about Wiley products, visit our web site at www.wiley.com.

Library of Congress Cataloging-in-Publication Data:

Bogle, John C.
The little book of common sense investing : the only way to guarantee
  your fair share of stock market returns / John C. Bogle.
    p. cm.
  ISBN-13: 978-0-470-10210-7 (cloth)
  ISBN-10: 0-470-10210-1 (cloth)
  1. Index mutual funds. I. Title.
  HG4530.B635 2007
  332.63'27—dc22

2006037552

Printed in the United States of America.

10 9 8 7 6 5 4 3 2 1

To Paul A. Samuelson, professor of economics
at Massachusetts Institute of Technology,
Nobel Laureate, investment sage.
In 1948 when I was a student at Princeton
University, his classic textbook introduced me
to economics. In 1974, his writings reignited my
interest in market indexing as an investment strategy.
In 1976, his *Newsweek* column applauded my creation of the world's first index mutual fund. In
1993, he wrote the foreword to my first book, and
in 1999 he provided a powerful endorsement for my
second. Now in his ninety-second year, he remains
my mentor, my inspiration, my shining light.

Contents

Chapter Five
The Grand Illusion

Chapter Six
Taxes Are Costs, Too

Chapter Seven
When the Good Times No Longer Roll

Chapter Eight
Selecting Long-Term Winners

Chapter Nine
Yesterday's Winners, Tomorrow's Losers

Chapter Ten
Seeking Advice to Select Funds?

Chapter Eleven
Focus on the Lowest-Cost Funds

Chapter Twelve
Profit from the Majesty of Simplicity

Introduction

~

Don't Allow a Winner's Game to Become a Loser's Game.

SUCCESSFUL INVESTING IS ALL about common sense. As the Oracle has said, it is simple, but it is not easy. Simple arithmetic suggests, and history confirms, that the winning strategy is to own all of the nation's publicly held businesses at very low cost. By doing so you are guaranteed to capture almost the entire return that they generate in the form of dividends and earnings growth.

The best way to implement this strategy is indeed simple: Buying a fund that holds this market portfolio, and holding it forever. Such a fund is called an index fund. The index fund is simply a basket (portfolio) that holds many, many eggs (stocks) designed to mimic the overall performance of any financial market or market sector.* Classic index funds, by definition, basically represent the entire stock market basket, not just a few scattered eggs. Such funds eliminate the risk of individual stocks, the risk of market sectors, and the risk of manager selection, with only stock market risk remaining (which is quite large enough, thank you). Index funds make up for their short-term lack of excitement by their truly exciting long-term productivity.

$\sim$

Index funds eliminate the risks of individual stocks, market sectors, and manager selection. Only stock market risk remains.

This is much more than a book about index funds. It is a book that is determined to change the very way that you think about investing. For when you understand how our financial markets actually work, you will see that the index fund is indeed the only investment that guarantees you will capture your fair share of the returns that business earns. Thanks to the miracle of compounding, the

---

* Keep in mind that an index may also be constructed around bonds and the bond market, or even "road less traveled" asset classes such as commodities or real estate. Today, if you wish, you could literally hold all your wealth in a diversified set of index funds representing asset classes within the United States or the global economy.

accumulations of wealth over the years generated by those returns have been little short of fantastic.

I'm speaking here about the classic index fund, one that is broadly diversified, holding all (or almost all) of its share of the $15 trillion capitalization of the U.S. stock market, operating with minimal expenses and without advisory fees, with tiny portfolio turnover, and with high tax efficiency. The index fund simply owns corporate America, buying an interest in each stock in the stock market in proportion to its market capitalization and then holding it forever.

Please don't underestimate the power of compounding the generous returns earned by our businesses. Over the past century, our corporations have earned a return on their capital of 9.5 percent per year. Compounded at that rate over a decade, each $1 initially invested grows to $2.48; over two decades, $6.14; over three decades, $15.22; over four decades, $37.72, and over five decades, $93.48.* The magic of compounding is little short of a miracle. Simply put, thanks to the growth, productivity, resourcefulness, and innovation of our corporations, capitalism creates

---

* These accumulations are measured in *nominal* dollars, with no adjustment for the long-term decline in their buying power, averaging about 3 percent a year since the twentieth century began. If we use real (inflation-adjusted) dollars, the return drops from 9.5 percent to 6.5 percent. As a result, the accumulations of an initial investment of $1 would be $1.88, $3.52, $6.61, $12.42, and $23.31 for the respective periods.

wealth, a *positive-sum game* for its owners. *Investing in equities is a winner's game.*

The returns earned by business are ultimately translated into the returns earned by the stock market. I have no way of knowing what share of these returns you have earned in the past. But academic studies suggest that if you are a typical investor in individual stocks, your returns have probably lagged the market by about 2.5 percentage points per year. Applying that figure to the annual return of 12 percent earned over the past 25 years by the Standard & Poor's 500 Stock Index, your annual return has been less than 10 percent. Result: your slice of the market pie, as it were, has been less than 80 percent. In addition, as explained in Chapter 5, if you are a typical investor in mutual funds, you've done even worse.

If you don't believe that is what most investors experience, please think for a moment, about the relentless rules of humble arithmetic. These iron rules define the game. As investors, all of us as a group earn the stock market's return. As a group—I hope you're sitting down for this astonishing revelation—we are average. Each extra return that one of us earns means that another of our fellow investors suffers a return shortfall of precisely the same dimension. *Before the deduction of the costs of investing, beating the stock market is a zero-sum game.*

But the costs of playing the investment game both reduce the gains of the winners and increases the losses of the losers. So who wins? You know who wins. The man in the middle (actually, the men and women in the middle, the brokers, the investment bankers, the money managers, the marketers, the lawyers, the accountants, the operations departments of our financial system) is the only sure winner in the game of investing. *Our financial croupiers always win.* In the casino, the house always wins. In horse racing, the track always wins. In the powerball lottery, the state always wins. Investing is no different. *After the deduction of the costs of investing, beating the stock market is a loser's game.*

Yes, after the costs of financial intermediation—all those brokerage commissions, portfolio transaction costs, and fund operating expenses; all those investment management fees; all those advertising dollars and all those marketing schemes; and all those legal costs and custodial fees that we pay, day after day and year after year—beating the market is inevitably a game for losers. No matter how many books are published and promoted purporting to show how easy it is to win, investors fall short. Indeed, when we add the costs of these self-help investment books into the equation, it becomes even more of a loser's game.

~

Don't allow a winner's game to become a loser's game.

The wonderful *magic of compounding returns* that is reflected in the long-term productivity of American business, then, is translated into equally wonderful returns in the stock market. But those returns are overwhelmed by the powerful *tyranny of compounding* the *costs* of investing. For those who choose to play the game, the odds in favor of the successful achievement of superior returns are terrible. Simply playing the game consigns the average investor to a woeful shortfall to the returns generated by the stock market over the long term.

Most investors in stocks think that they can avoid the pitfalls of investing by due diligence and knowledge, trading stocks with alacrity to stay one step ahead of the game. But while the investors who trade the least have a fighting chance of capturing the market's return, those who trade the most are doomed to failure. An academic study showed that the most active one-fifth of all stock traders turned their portfolios over at the rate of more than 21 percent per month. While they earned the market return of 17.9 percent per year during the period 1990 to 1996, they incurred trading costs of about 6.5 percent, leaving them with an annual return of but 11.4

percent, only two-thirds of the return in that strong market upsurge.

Fund investors are confident that they can easily select superior fund managers. They are wrong.

Mutual fund investors, too, have inflated ideas of their own omniscience. They pick funds based on the recent performance superiority of fund managers, or even their long-term superiority, and hire advisers to help them do the same thing. But, the advisers do it with even less success (see Chapters 8, 9, and 10). Oblivious of the toll taken by costs, fund investors willingly pay heavy sales loads and incur excessive fund fees and expenses, and are unknowingly subjected to the substantial but hidden transaction costs incurred by funds as a result of their hyperactive portfolio turnover. Fund investors are confident that they can easily select superior fund managers. They are wrong.

Contrarily, for those who invest and then drop out of the game and never pay a single unnecessary cost, the odds in favor of success are awesome. Why? Simply because they own *businesses,* and businesses as a group earn substantial returns on their capital and pay out dividends to their owners. Yes, many individual companies fail. Firms with flawed ideas and rigid strategies and weak managements ultimately fall victim to the *creative destruction* that is the hallmark of competitive capitalism, only to be succeeded by others.* But in the aggregate, businesses grow with the long-term growth of our vibrant economy.

This book will tell you why you should stop contributing to the croupiers of the financial markets, who rake in something like $400 billion each year from you and your fellow investors. It will also tell you how easy it is to do just that: simply buy the entire stock market. Then, once you have bought your stocks, get out of the casino and stay out. Just hold the market portfolio forever. And that's what the index fund does.

This investment philosophy is not only simple and elegant. The arithmetic on which it is based is irrefutable. But it is not easy to follow its discipline. So long as we investors accept the status quo of today's crazy-quilt financial market system; so long as we enjoy the excitement (however costly) of buying and selling stocks; so long as we fail to realize that there is a better way, such a philosophy will seem counterintuitive. But I ask you to carefully consider the impassioned message of this little book. When you do, you, too, will want to join the revolution and invest in a new, more economical, more efficient, even more honest way, a more productive way that will put your own interest first.

* "Creative destruction" is the formulation of Joseph E. Schumpeter in *Capitalism, Socialism, and Democracy,* 1942.

It may seem farfetched for me to hope that any single little book could ignite the spark of a revolution in investing. New ideas that fly in the face of the conventional wisdom of the day are always greeted with doubt, scorn, and even fear. Indeed, 230 years ago the same challenge was faced by Thomas Paine, whose 1776 tract *Common Sense* helped spark the American Revolution. Here is what Tom Paine wrote:

> Perhaps the sentiments contained in the following pages are not yet sufficiently fashionable to procure them general favor; a long habit of not thinking a thing wrong, gives it a superficial appearance of being right, and raises at first a formidable outcry in defense of custom. But the tumult soon subsides. Time makes more converts than reason.
>
> In the following pages, I offer nothing more than simple facts, plain arguments, and common sense; and have no other preliminaries to settle with the reader, than that he will divest himself of prejudice and prepossession, and suffer his reason and his feelings to determine for themselves; that he will put on, or rather that he will not put off, the true character of a man, and generously enlarge his views beyond the present day.

As we now know, Thomas Paine's powerful and articulate arguments carried the day. The American Revolution led to our Constitution, which to this day defines the responsibility of our government, our citizens, and the fabric of our society. Inspired by his words, I titled my

1999 book *Common Sense on Mutual Funds,* and asked investors to divest themselves of prejudice and to generously enlarge their views beyond the present day. In this new book, I reiterate that proposition.

If I "could only explain things to enough people, carefully enough, thoroughly enough, thoughtfully enough—why, eventually everyone would see, and then everything would be fixed."

In *Common Sense on Mutual Funds,* I also applied to my idealistic self these words of the late journalist Michael Kelly: "The driving dream (of the idealist) is that if he could only explain things to enough people, carefully enough, thoroughly enough, thoughtfully enough—why, eventually everyone would see, and then everything would be fixed." This book is my attempt to explain the financial system to as many of you who will listen carefully enough, thoroughly enough, and thoughtfully enough so that you will see, and it will be fixed. Or at least that your own participation in it will be fixed.

Some may suggest that, as the creator both of Vanguard in 1974 and of the world's first index mutual fund in 1975, I have a vested interest in persuading you of my views. Of course I do! But not because it enriches me to do so. It doesn't earn me a penny. Rather, I want to persuade you because the very elements that formed Vanguard's foundation all those years ago—all those values and structures and strategies—will enrich *you*.

In the early years of indexing, my voice was a lonely one. But there were a few other thoughtful and respected believers whose ideas inspired me to carry on my mission. Today, many of the wisest and most successful investors endorse the index fund concept, and among academics, the acceptance is close to universal. *But don't take my word for it.* Listen to these independent experts with no axe to grind except for the truth about investing. You'll hear from some of them at the end of each chapter.

Listen, for example, to this endorsement by Paul A. Samuelson, Nobel Laureate and professor of economics at Massachusetts Institute of Technology, to whom this book is dedicated: "Bogle's reasoned precepts can enable a few million of us savers to become in twenty years the envy of our suburban neighbors—while at the same time we have slept well in these eventful times."

Put another way, in the words of the Shaker hymn, "Tis the gift to be simple, tis the gift to be free, tis the gift to come down where we ought to be." Adapting this message to investing by simply owning an index fund, you will be free of almost all of the excessive costs of our financial system, and will receive, when it comes time to draw on the savings you have accumulated, the gift of coming down just where you ought to be.

The financial system, alas, won't be fixed for a long time. But the glacial nature of that change doesn't prevent you from looking after your self-interest. You don't need to participate in its expensive foolishness. If you choose to play the winner's game of owning businesses and refrain from playing the loser's game of trying to beat the market, you can begin the task simply by using your own common sense, understanding the system, and investing in accordance with the only principles that will eliminate substantially all of its excessive costs. Then, at last, whatever returns our businesses may be generous enough to deliver in the years ahead, reflected as they will be in our stock and bond markets, you will be guaranteed to earn your fair share. When you understand these realities, you'll see that it's all about common sense.

JOHN C. BOGLE

Valley Forge, Pennsylvania
January 5, 2007

Don't Take My Word for It

Charles T. Munger, Warren Buffett's partner at Berkshire Hathaway, puts it this way: "The general systems of money management [today] require people to pretend to do something they can't do and like something they don't. [It's] a funny business because on a net basis, the whole investment management business together gives no value added to all buyers combined. *That's the way it has to work.* Mutual funds charge two percent per year and then brokers switch people between funds, costing another three to four percentage points. The poor guy in the general public is getting a terrible product from the professionals. I think it's disgusting. It's much better to be part of a system that delivers value to the people who buy the product."

William Bernstein, investment adviser (and neurologist), and author of *The Four Pillars of Investing,* says: "It's bad enough that you have to take market risk. Only a fool takes on the additional risk of doing yet more damage by failing to diversify properly with his or her nest egg. Avoid the problem—buy a well-run index fund and own the whole market."

Here's how the *Economist* of London puts it: "The truth is that, for the most part, fund managers have offered extremely poor value for money. Their

(continued)

records of outperformance are almost always followed by stretches of underperformance. Over long periods of time, hardly any fund managers have beaten the market averages. They encourage investors, rather than spread their risks wisely or seek the best match for their future liabilities, to put their money into the most modish assets going, often just when they become overvalued. And all the while they charge their clients big fees for the privilege of losing their money. . . . (One) specific lesson . . . is the merits of indexed investing . . . you will almost never find a fund manager who can repeatedly beat the market. It is better to invest in an indexed fund that promises a market return but with significantly lower fees."

The Little Book readers interested in reviewing the original sources for the "Don't Take My Word for It" quotes, found at the end of each chapter, and other quotes in the main text, can find them on my website: www.johncbogle.com. I wouldn't dream of consuming valuable pages in this book with a weighty bibliography, so please don't hesitate to visit my website. It's really amazing that so many giants of academe and many of the world's greatest investors, known for beating the market, confirm and applaud the virtues of index investing. May their common sense, perhaps even more than my own, make you all wiser investors.

A Parable

~

The Gotrocks Family

EVEN BEFORE YOU THINK about "index funds"—
in their most basic form, mutual funds that simply buy
all the stocks in the U.S. stock market and hold them
forever—you must understand how the stock market
actually works. Perhaps this homely parable—my ver-
sion of a story told by Warren Buffett, chairman
of Berkshire Hathaway Inc., in the firm's 2005
Annual Report—will clarify the foolishness and coun-
terproductivity of our vast and complex financial market system.

Once upon a Time ...

A wealthy family named the Gotrocks, grown over the generations to include thousands of brothers, sisters, aunts, uncles, and cousins, owned 100 percent of every stock in the United States. Each year, they reaped the rewards of investing: all the earnings growth that those thousands of corporations generated and all the dividends that they distributed.* Each family member grew wealthier at the same pace, and all was harmonious. Their investment had compounded over the decades, creating enormous wealth, because the Gotrocks family was playing a winner's game.

But after a while, a few fast-talking Helpers arrive on the scene, and they persuade some "smart" Gotrocks cousins that they can earn a larger share than the other relatives. These Helpers convince the cousins to sell some of their shares in the companies to other family members and to buy some shares of others from them in return. The Helpers handle the transactions, and as brokers, they receive commissions for their services. The ownership is thus rearranged among the family members.

To their surprise, however, the family wealth begins to grow at a slower pace. Why? Because some of the return is now consumed by the Helpers, and the family's share of the

---

* To complicate matters just a bit, the Gotrocks family also purchased the new public offerings of securities that were issued each year.

generous pie that U.S. industry bakes each year—all those dividends paid, all those earnings reinvested in the business—100 percent at the outset, starts to decline, simply because some of the return is now consumed by the Helpers.

To make matters worse, while the family had always paid taxes on their dividends, some of the members are now also paying taxes on the capital gains they realize from their stock-swapping back and forth, further diminishing the family's total wealth.

The smart cousins quickly realize that their plan has actually diminished the rate of growth in the family's wealth. They recognize that their foray into stock-picking has been a failure and conclude that they need professional assistance, the better to pick the right stocks for themselves. So they hire stock-picking experts—more Helpers!—to gain an advantage. These money managers charge a fee for their services. So when the family appraises its wealth a year later, it finds that its share of the pie has diminished even further.

To make matters still worse, the new managers feel compelled to earn their keep by trading the family's stocks at feverish levels of activity, not only increasing the brokerage commissions paid to the first set of Helpers, but running up the tax bill as well. Now the family's earlier 100 percent share of the dividend and earnings pie is further diminished.

"Well, we failed to pick good stocks for ourselves, and when that didn't work, we also failed to pick managers who could do so," the smart cousins say. "What shall we do?" Undeterred by their two previous failures, they decide to hire still more Helpers. They retain the best investment consultants and financial planners they can find to advise them on how to select the right managers, who will then surely pick the right stocks. The consultants, of course, tell them they can do exactly that. "Just pay us a fee for our services," the new Helpers assure the cousins, "and all will be well." Alas, the family's share of the pie tumbles once again.

Get rid of all your Helpers. Then our family will again reap 100 percent of the pie that Corporate America bakes for us.

Alarmed at last, the family sits down together and takes stock of the events that have transpired since some of them began to try to outsmart the others. "How is it," they ask, "that our original 100 percent share of the pie—made up each year of all those dividends and earnings—has dwindled to just 60 percent?" Their wisest member, a sage old uncle, softly responds: "All that money you've paid to those Helpers and all those unnecessary extra taxes you're paying come directly out of our family's total earnings and dividends. *Go back to square one, and do so immediately.* Get rid of all your brokers. Get rid of all your money managers. Get rid of all your consultants. Then our family will again reap 100 percent of however large a pie that corporate America bakes for us, year after year."

They followed the old uncle's wise advice, returning to their original passive but productive strategy, holding all the stocks of corporate America, and standing pat. That is exactly what an index fund does.

. . . and the Gotrocks Family Lived Happily Ever After

Adding a fourth law to Sir Isaac Newton's three laws of motion, the inimitable Warren Buffett puts the moral of the story this way: *For investors as a whole, returns decrease as motion increases.*

Accurate as that cryptic statement is, I would add that the parable reflects the profound conflict of interest between those who work in the investment business and those who invest in stocks and bonds. The way to wealth for those in the business is to persuade their clients, *"Don't just stand there. Do something."* But the way to wealth for their clients in the aggregate is to follow the opposite maxim: *"Don't do something. Just stand there."* For that is the only way to avoid playing the loser's game of trying to beat the market. When any business is conducted in a way that directly defies the interests of its clients in the aggregate, it is only a matter of time until change comes.

The moral of the story, then, is that successful investing is about owning businesses and reaping the huge rewards provided by the dividends and earnings growth of our nation's—and, for that matter, the world's—corporations. *The higher the level of their investment activity, the greater the cost of financial intermediation and taxes, the less the net return that the business owners as a group receive.* The lower the costs that investors as a group incur, the higher rewards that they reap. So to realize the winning returns generated by businesses over the long term, the intelligent investor will minimize to the bare bones the costs of financial intermediation. That's what common sense tells us. That's what indexing is all about. And that's what this book is all about.

Don't Take My Word for It

Listen to **Jack R. Meyer,** former president of Harvard Management Company, the remarkably successful wizard who tripled the Harvard endowment fund from $8 billion to $27 billion. Here's what he had to say in a 2004 *Business Week* interview: "The investment business is a giant scam. Most people think they can find managers who can outperform, but most people are wrong. I will say that 85 to 90 percent of managers fail to match their benchmarks. Because managers have fees and incur transaction costs, you know that in the aggregate they are deleting value." When asked if private investors can draw any lessons from what Harvard does, Mr. Meyer responded, "Yes. First, get diversified. Come up with a portfolio that covers a lot of asset classes. Second, you want to keep your fees low. That means avoiding the most hyped but expensive funds, in favor of low-cost index funds. And finally, invest for the long term. [Investors] should simply have index funds to keep their fees low and their taxes down. *No doubt about it.*"

In terms that are a bit more academic, Princeton professor **Burton G. Malkiel,** author of *A Random Walk Down Wall Street,* expresses these views: "Index funds have regularly produced rates of return exceeding those of active managers by close to 2 percentage points. Active management as a whole cannot achieve gross returns exceeding the market as a while and therefore they must, on average, underperform the indexes by the amount of these expense and transaction costs disadvantages.

(continued)

"Experience conclusively shows that index-fund buyers are likely to obtain results exceeding those of the typical fund manager, whose large advisory fees and substantial portfolio turnover tend to reduce investment yields. Many people will find the guarantee of playing the stock-market game at par every round a very attractive one. The index fund is a sensible, serviceable method for obtaining the market's rate of return with absolutely no effort and minimal expense."

Chapter Two

Rational Exuberance

~

*Business Reality Trumps
Market Expectations.*

THAT WONDERFUL PARABLE ABOUT the Gotrocks family in Chapter 1 brings home the central reality of investing: "The most that owners in the aggregate can earn between now and Judgment Day is what their business in the aggregate earns," in the words of Warren Buffett. Illustrating the point with Berkshire Hathaway, the publicly owned investment company he has run for 40 years, Buffett says, "When the stock temporarily overperforms or underperforms the business, a limited number of shareholders—either sellers or buyers—receive out-sized benefits at the expense of those they trade with. *[But] over time, the aggregate gains made by Berkshire shareholders must of necessity match the business gains of the company."*

---------------- ◇ ----------------

"Over time, the aggregate gains made by shareholders must of necessity match the business gains of the company."

How often investors lose sight of that eternal principle! Yet the record is clear. History, if only we would take the trouble to look at it, reveals the remarkable, if essential, linkage between the cumulative long-term returns earned by *business*—the annual dividend yield plus the annual rate of earnings growth—and the cumulative returns earned by the U.S. *stock market*. Think about that certainty for a moment. Can you see that it is simple common sense?

Need proof? Just look at the record since the twentieth century began (Exhibit 2.1). The average annual total return on stocks was 9.6 percent, virtually identical to the investment return of 9.5 percent—4.5 percent from dividend yield and 5 percent from earnings growth. That tiny difference of 0.1 percent per year arose from what I call *speculative* return. Depending on how one looks at it, it is merely statistical noise, or perhaps it reflects a generally upward long-term trend in stock valuations, a willingness of investors to pay higher prices for each dollar of earnings at the end of the period than at the beginning.

EXHIBIT 2.1   Investment Return versus Market Return—Growth of $1, 1900–2005

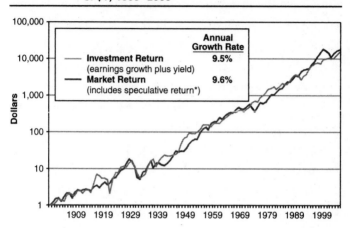

*Impact of change in price-earnings ratio.

Compounding these returns over 106 years produced accumulations that are truly staggering. Each dollar initially invested in 1900 at an investment return of 9.5 percent grew by the close of 2005 to $15,062.* Sure, few (if any) of us have 106 years in us, but, like the Gotrocks family over the generations, the miracle of compounding returns is little short of amazing—it is perhaps the ultimate winner's game.

*But let's be fair. If we compound that initial $1, not at the nominal return of 9.5 percent but at the real (after-inflation) rate of 6.5 percent, the accumulation grows to $793. But increasing real wealth nearly 800 times over is not to be sneezed at.

As Exhibit 2.1 makes clear, there are bumps along the way in the investment returns earned by our business corporations. Sometimes, as in the Great Depression of the early 1930s, these bumps are large. But we get over them. So, if you stand back from the chart and squint your eyes, the trend of business fundamentals looks almost like a straight line sloping gently upward, and those periodic bumps are barely visible.

Stock market returns sometimes get well ahead of business fundamentals (as in the late 1920s, the early 1970s, the late 1990s). But it has been only a matter of time until, as if drawn by a magnet, they soon return, although often only after falling well behind for a time (as in the mid-1940s, the late 1970s, the 2003 market lows).

In our foolish focus on the short-term stock market distractions of the moment, we, too, often overlook this long history. We ignore that when the returns on stocks depart materially from the long-term norm, it is rarely because of the *economics* of investing—the earnings growth and dividend yields of our corporations. Rather, the reason that annual stock returns are so volatile is largely because of the *emotions* of investing.

We can measure these emotions by the price/earnings (P/E) ratio, which measures the number of dollars investors are willing to pay for each dollar of earnings. As investor confidence waxes and wanes, P/E multiples rise and fall.* When greed holds sway, we see very high P/Es. When hope prevails, P/Es are moderate. When fear is in the saddle, P/Es are very low. Back and forth, over and over again, swings in the emotions of investors momentarily derail the steady long-range upward trend in the economics of investing.

"It is dangerous . . . to apply to the future inductive arguments based on past experience."

What Exhibit 2.1 shows is that while the prices we pay for stocks often lose touch with the reality of corporate values, *in the long run, reality rules.* So, while investors seem to intuitively accept that the past is inevitably prologue to the future, any past stock market returns that have included a high speculative stock return component are a deeply flawed guide to what lies ahead. To understand why past returns do not foretell the future, we need only heed the words of the great British economist John Maynard Keynes, written 70 years ago: "It is dangerous . . . to apply to the future inductive arguments based on past experience, unless one can distinguish the broad reasons why past experience was what it was."

*Changes in interest rates also have an impact, uneven though it may be, on the P/E multiple. So, I'm oversimplifying a bit here.

But if we can distinguish the reasons the past was what it was, then, we can establish reasonable expectations about the future. Keynes helped us make this distinction by pointing out that the state of long-term expectation for stocks is a combination of *enterprise* ("forecasting the prospective yield of assets over their whole life") and *speculation* ("forecasting the psychology of the market"). I'm well familiar with those words, for 55 years ago I incorporated them in my senior thesis at Princeton, written (providentially for my lifetime career that followed) on the mutual fund industry. It was entitled, "The Economic Role of the Investment Company."

This dual nature of returns is reflected when we look at stock market returns over the decades. Using Keynes's idea, I divide stock market returns into two parts: (1) *Investment Return* (enterprise), consisting of the initial dividend yield on stocks plus their subsequent earnings growth, which together form the essence of what we call "intrinsic value"; and (2) *Speculative Return,* the impact of changing price/earnings multiples on stock prices.

Let's begin with investment returns. Exhibit 2.2 shows the average annual investment return on stocks over the decades since 1900. Note first the steady contribution of dividend yields to total return during each decade; always positive, only once outside the range of 3 percent to 7 percent, and averaging 4.5 percent. Then note that the con-

EXHIBIT 2.2   Investment Return by the Decade (Percentage/Year)

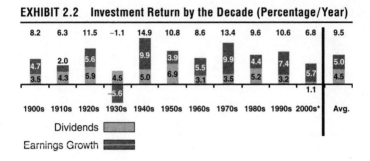

| 8.2 | 6.3 | 11.5 | −1.1 | 14.9 | 10.8 | 8.6 | 13.4 | 9.6 | 10.6 | 6.8 | 9.5 |

Dividends
Earnings Growth

Example: In the 1980s, the P/E multiple rose from 7.3 to 15.2 times, a 110 percent increase, equal to 7.7 percent per year.
*2000–2005 inclusive.

tribution of earnings growth to investment return, with the exception of the depression-ridden 1930s, was positive in every decade, usually running between 4 percent and 7 percent, and averaging 5 percent per year. Result: Total *investment* returns (the top line, combining dividend yield and earnings growth) were negative in only a single decade (again, in the 1930s). These total investment returns—the gains made by business—were remarkably steady, generally running in the range of 8 percent to 13 percent each year, and averaging 9.5 percent.

Enter speculative return. Compared with the relative consistency of dividends and earnings growth over the decades, truly wild variations in speculative return punctuate the chart as price/earnings ratios (P/Es) wax and wane (Exhibit 2.3). A 100 percent rise in the P/E, from

EXHIBIT 2.3   Speculative Return by the Decade (Percentage/Year)

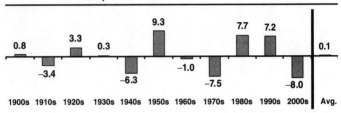

10 to 20 times over a decade, would equate to a 7.2 percent annual speculative return. Curiously, without exception, every decade of significantly negative speculative return was immediately followed by a decade in which it turned positive by a correlative amount—the quiet 1910s and then the roaring 1920s, the dispiriting 1940s and then the booming 1950s, the discouraging 1970s and then the soaring 1980s—reversion to the mean (RTM) writ large. (Reversion to the mean can be thought of as the tendency for stock returns to return to their long-term norms over time—periods of exceptional returns tend to be followed by periods of below average performance, and vice versa.) Then, amazingly, there is an unprecedented second consecutive exuberant increase in speculative return in the 1990s, a pattern never before in evidence.

By the close of 1999, the P/E rate had risen to an unprecedented level 32 times, setting the stage for the return to sanity in valuations that soon followed. The tumble in stock market prices gave us our comeuppance. With earnings continuing to rise, the P/E currently stands at 18 times, compared with the 15 times level that prevailed at the start of the twentieth century. As a result, speculative return has added just 0.1 percentage points to the annual investment return earned by our businesses over the long term.

When we combine these two sources of stock returns, we get the total return produced by the stock market (Exhibit 2.4). Despite the huge impact of speculative

EXHIBIT 2.4   Total Stock Return by the Decade (Percentage/Year)

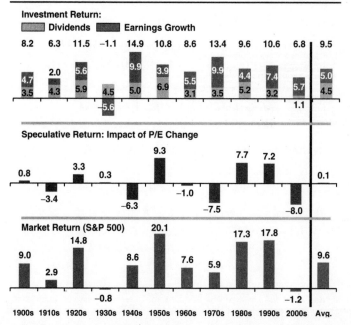

return—up and down—during most of the individual decades, there is virtually *no* impact over the long term. The average annual total return on stocks of 9.6 percent, then, has been created almost entirely by *enterprise,* with only 0.1 percentage point created by *speculation.* The message is clear: in the long run, stock returns depend almost entirely on the reality of the investment returns earned by our corporations. The perception of investors, reflected by the speculative returns, counts for little. It is economics that controls long-term equity returns; emotions, so dominant in the short-term, dissolve.

Accurately forecasting swings in investor emotions is not possible. But forecasting the long-term economics of investing carries remarkably high odds of success.

After more than 55 years in this business, I have absolutely no idea how to forecast these swings in investor emotions.* But, largely because the arithmetic of investing is so basic, I can forecast the long-term economics of investing with remarkably high odds of success. Why? Simply, it is

---

* I'm not alone. I don't know anyone who has done so successfully, or even anyone who knows anyone who has done so. In fact, 70 years of financial research show that no one has done so.

investment returns—the earnings and dividends generated by American business—that are almost entirely responsible for the returns delivered in our stock market. Put another way, while illusion (the momentary prices we pay for stocks) often loses touch with reality (the intrinsic values of our corporations), in the long run it is reality that rules.

To drive this point home, think of investing as consisting of two different games. Here's how Roger Martin, dean of the Rotman School of Management of the University of Toronto, describes them. One is "the *real* market, where giant publicly held companies compete. Where real companies spend real money to make and sell real products and services, and, if they play with skill, earn real profits and pay real dividends. This game also requires real strategy, determination, and expertise; real innovation and real foresight."

Loosely linked to this game is another game, the *expectations* market. Here, "prices are not set by real things like sales margins or profits. In the short-term, stock prices go up only when the expectations of investors rise, not necessarily when sales, margins, or profits rise."

The stock market is a giant distraction.

To this crucial distinction, I would add that the expectations market is not only a product of the expectations of active investors but the expectations of active speculators, trying to guess what these investors will expect, and how they will act as each new bit of information finds its way into the marketplace. *The expectations market is about speculation. The real market is about investing.* The only logical conclusion: the stock market is a giant distraction that causes investors to focus on transitory and volatile investment expectations rather than on what is really important—the gradual accumulation of the returns earned by corporate business.

My advice to investors is to ignore the short-term noise of the emotions reflected in our financial markets and focus on the productive long-term economics of our corporate businesses. Shakespeare could have been describing the inexplicable hourly and daily—sometimes even yearly or longer—fluctuations in the stock market when he wrote, "[It is] like a tale told by an idiot, full of sound and fury, signifying nothing." The way to investment success is to get out of the expectations market of stock prices and cast your lot with the real market of business.

Don't Take My Word for It

Simply heed the timeless distinction made by **Benjamin Graham**, legendary investor, author of *The Intelligent Investor* and mentor to Warren Buffett. He was right on the money when he put his finger on the essential reality of investing: *"In the short run the stock market is a voting machine . . . (but) in the long run it is a weighing machine."* Ben Graham continues, using his wonderful metaphor of "Mr. Market." "The investor with a portfolio of sound stocks should expect their prices to fluctuate and should neither be concerned by sizable declines nor become excited by sizable advances. He should always remember that market quotations are there for his convenience, either to be taken advantage of or to be ignored.

"Imagine that in some private business you own a small share which cost you $1,000. One of your partners, named Mr. Market, is very obliging indeed. Every day he tells you what he thinks your interest is worth and furthermore offers either to buy you out or to sell you an additional interest on that basis. Sometimes his idea of value appears plausible and justified by business developments and prospects. Often, on the other hand, Mr. Market lets his enthusiasm or his fears run away with him, and the value he proposes seems little short of silly.

"If you are a prudent investor will you let Mr. Market's daily communication determine your view as the value of your $1,000 interest in the enterprise? Only in case you agree with him or in case you want to trade with him. Most of the time you

(continued)

will be wiser to form your own ideas of the value of your holdings. The true investor . . . will do better *if he forgets about the stock market and pays attention to his dividend returns and to the operating results of his companies.*"

Chapter Three

Cast Your Lot
with Business

∽

Rely on Occam's Razor
to Win by Keeping It Simple.

So how do you cast your lot with business? Simply by buying a portfolio that owns the shares of every business in the United States and then holding it forever. It is a simple concept that guarantees you will win the investment game played by most other investors who—as a group—are guaranteed to lose.

Please don't equate simplicity with stupidity. Way back in 1320, William of Occam expressed it well, essentially setting forth this precept: When there are multiple solutions to a problem, choose the simplest one.* And so *Occam's Razor* came to represent a major principle of scientific inquiry. By far the simplest way to own all of U.S. business is to hold the total stock market portfolio.

~

Occam's Razor: When there are multiple solutions to a problem, choose the simplest one.

For most of the past 80 years, the accepted stock market portfolio was represented by the Standard & Poor's 500 Index (the S&P 500), which was created in 1926 and now lists 500 stocks. It is essentially composed of the 500 largest U.S. corporations, weighted by the value of their market capitalizations.† In recent years, these 500 stocks have represented about 80 percent of the market value of all U.S. stocks. The beauty of such a *cap-weighted* index is that it automatically adjusts to changing stock prices and never has to buy and sell stocks for that reason.

With the enormous growth of corporate pension funds between 1950 and 1990, it was an ideal measurement standard, the benchmark or hurdle rate that would be the comparative standard for how their professional managers were performing. Today, the S&P 500 remains a valid standard

---

* William of Occam expressed it more elegantly: "Entities should not be multiplied unnecessarily." But the point is unmistakable.
† The S&P Index originally included just 90 companies, rising to 500 in 1957.

against which to compare the returns earned by the professional managers of pension funds and mutual funds.

In 1970, an even more comprehensive measure of the U.S. stock market was developed. Originally called the Wilshire 5000, it is now named the Dow Jones Wilshire Total Stock Market Index. It includes some 4,971 stocks, including the 500 stocks in the S&P 500. However, because its component stocks also are weighted by their market capitalization, those remaining 4,471 stocks account for only about 20 percent of its value. Nonetheless, this broadest of all U.S. stock indexes is the best measure of the aggregate value of stocks, and therefore a superb measure of the returns earned in U.S. stocks by all investors as a group.

The two indexes have a similar composition. Exhibit 3.1 shows the 12 largest stocks in each, and their weight in the construction of each index.

Given the similarity of these two portfolios, it is hardly surprising that the two indexes have earned returns that are in lockstep with one another. The Center for Research in Security Prices at the University of Chicago has gone back to 1926 and calculated the returns earned by all U.S. stocks. (Its data since 1970 have provided a virtually perfect match to the Total Stock Market Index.) In fact, returns of the two indexes parallel one another with near precision. From 1928, the beginning of the measurement period, through 2006, you can hardly tell them apart (Exhibit 3.2).

EXHIBIT 3.1 S&P 500 versus Total Stock Market Index: Portfolio Comparison, July 2006

| S&P 500 | | Total Stock Market Index | |
Rank	Weighting	Rank	Weighting
1. Exxon Mobil	3.2%	1. Exxon Mobil	2.6%
2. General Electric	3.0	2. General Electric	2.4
3. Citigroup	2.1	3. Citigroup	1.7
4. Bank of America	1.9	4. Bank of America	1.5
5. Microsoft	1.8	5. Microsoft	1.5
6. Procter & Gamble	1.6	6. Procter & Gamble	1.3
7. Johnson & Johnson	1.5	7. Johnson & Johnson	1.2
8. Pfizer	1.5	8. Pfizer	1.2
9. American International Group	1.3	9. Altria Group	1.1
10. Altria Group	1.3	10. J.P. Morgan	1.0
11. J.P. Morgan	1.3	11. Chevron	1.0
12. Chevron	1.2	12. American International Group	0.9
Top 12	21.7%	Top 12	17.1%
Top 25	33.5	Top 25	26.3
Top 100	64.3	Top 100	50.5
Top 500	100.0	Top 500	81.0
Total market cap	$11.9 trillion	Total market cap	$15 trillion

EXHIBIT 3.2   S&P 500 and the Total Stock Market Index

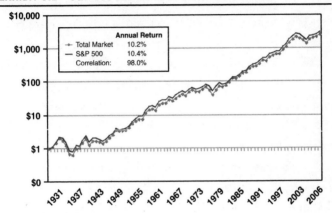

For the full period, the average annual return on the S&P 500 was 10.3 percent; the return on the Total Stock Market Index was 10.1 percent. This represents what we call a *period dependent* outcome—everything depends on the starting date and the ending date. If we were to begin the comparison at the beginning of 1930 instead of 1926, the returns of the two would be identical: 9.9 percent per year.

Yes, there are variations over the interim periods: the S&P 500 was much the stronger from 1982 to 1990, when its annual return of 15.6 percent outpaced the Total Stock Market Index return of 14.0 percent. But in recent years (1998 to 2006), small- and mid-cap stocks did better, and the Total Stock Market Index return of 3.4 percent per year nicely exceeded the 2.4 percent return of the S&P 500. But with a long-term correlation of 0.98 between the returns of the two indexes (1.0 is perfect correlation), there is little to choose between them.

Whichever measure we use, it should now be obvious that the returns earned by the publicly held corporations that compose the stock market must of necessity equal the aggregate gross returns earned by all investors in that market as a group. Equally obvious, as discussed in Chapter 4, the net returns earned by these investors must of necessity fall short of those aggregate gross returns by the amount of intermediation costs they incur. Our common sense tells us the obvious; while *owning* the stock market over the long term is a winner's game, *beating* the stock market is a loser's game.

If the data do not prove that indexing wins, well, the data are wrong.

Such an all-market fund is guaranteed to outpace over time the returns earned by equity investors as a group. Once you recognize this fact, you can see that the index fund is guaranteed to win not only over time, but every year, and every month and week, even every minute of the day. Because no matter how long or short the time frame, the gross return in the stock market, minus intermediation costs, equals the net return earned by investors as a group. If the data do not prove that indexing wins, well, the data are wrong.

Over the short term, however, it doesn't always look as if the S&P 500 (still the most common basis of comparison for mutual funds and pension plans) or the Total Stock Market Index is winning. That is because there is no possible way to calculate the returns earned by the millions of diverse participants, amateur and professional alike, Americans and foreign investors, in the U.S. stock market.

So what we do in the mutual fund field is calculate the returns of the various funds, counting each fund— instead of each fund's assets—as one entry. Since there are many small-cap and mid-cap funds, usually with relatively modest asset bases, they make a disproportionate impact on the data. When small- and mid-cap funds are leading the total market, the all-market index fund seems to lag. When small- and mid-cap stocks are lagging the market, the index fund looks formidable indeed.

Nonetheless, the exercise of calculating how the returns earned by the stock market compare with returns earned by the average equity fund is both illuminating and persuasive (Exhibit 3.3). If we compare the results of what are described as "large-cap core" funds with the returns of the S&P 500 (because of its market capitalization weightings, a "large-cap core" index), the advantage of the S&P Index is impressive.

EXHIBIT 3.3   Large-Cap Core Funds Outperformed by S&P 500

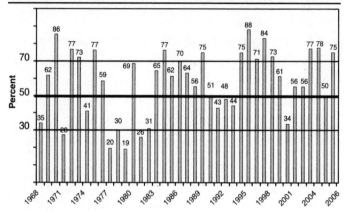

During the 39-year period 1968 to 2006, the S&P 500 fell into the bottom quartile in only two years (and has not done so since 1979). The Index has outpaced the average fund in 26 of the remaining 35 years, including 11 of the past 15 years. Its average ranking was in the 58th percentile (outperforming 58 percent of the comparable actively managed funds), leading, as we will show in Chapter 4, to enormous superiority over time. It is hard to imagine that even a single one of the large-cap core equity funds has a similar record of consistency.

Consistency matters. A fund that is good or very good in the vast majority of years produces a far larger long-term return than a fund that is superb in half the years and a disaster in the remaining half. Single-year rankings, then, ignore the sheer arithmetic advantage of that consistency. In the next chapter, the impact of that long-term consistency is catalogued over the past 25 years.

These annual data are what we call *survivor-biased;* they exclude the records of the inevitably poorer performing funds that regularly go out of business. As a result of this noise in the data, the chart further understates the success of the market-owning index strategy.

Much criticism has been heaped on the S&P 500 for often picking "new economy" stocks such as JDS Uniphase and Yahoo! near their inflated peak prices during the bubble, just before they crashed, thereby taking on a growth bias at exactly the wrong time. While the criticism is valid, the excellent long-term record of the flawed Index belies the existence of a significant problem. In fact, since the market peaked early in 2000 (as shown in Exhibit 3.3), the S&P 500 has had only a single significantly subpar year (2000), three years at about par, and three years (2003, 2004, and 2006) in the top quartile of its peers. I imagine that the vast majority of money managers would have been ecstatic with such an outcome.

***

The record of the first index mutual fund: $15,000 invested in 1976; value in 2006, $461,771.

Thus, the recent era not only has failed to erode, but has nicely enhanced the lifetime record of the world's first index fund—now known as Vanguard 500 Index Fund. Let me be specific: at a dinner on September 20, 2006, celebrating the 30th anniversary of the fund's initial public offering, the counsel for the fund's underwriters reported that he had purchased 1,000 shares at the original offering price of $15.00 per share—a $15,000 investment. He proudly announced that the value of his holding that evening (including shares acquired through reinvesting the fund's dividends and distributions over the years) was $461,771. Now, there's a number that requires no comment.*

This cumulative long-term winning record confirms that owning American business through a broadly diversified index fund is not only logical but, to say the least, incredibly productive. Equally important, it is consistent with the age-old principle expressed by Sir William of Occam: instead of joining the crowd of investors who dabble in complex machinations to pick stocks and try to outguess the stock market (two inevitably fruitless tasks for investors in the aggregate), choose the simplest of all solutions—buy and hold the market portfolio.

---

*Well, maybe one comment. Of the 360 equity mutual funds then in existence, only 211 remain.

Don't Take My Word for It

Hear **David Swensen,** widely respected chief investment officer of the Yale University Endowment Fund. "A minuscule 4 percent of funds produce market-beating after-tax results with a scant 0.6 percent (annual) margin of gain. The 96 percent of funds that fail to meet or beat the Vanguard 500 Index Fund lose by a wealth-destroying margin of 4.8 percent per annum."

The simple index fund solution has been adopted as a cornerstone of investment strategy for many of the nation's pension plans operated by our giant corporations and state and local governments. Indexing is also the predominant strategy for the largest of them all, the retirement plan for federal government employees, the **Federal Thrift Savings Plan** (TSP). The plan has been a remarkable success, and now holds some $173 billion of assets for the benefit of our public servants and members of armed services. All contributions and earnings are tax-deferred until withdrawal, much like the corporate 401(k) thrift plans. (Overcoming what must have been some serious reservations, even the Bush administration determined to follow the TSP model in its plan for Personal Savings Accounts as an optional alternative to our Social Security program.)

(continued)

Indexing is also praised across the Atlantic "pond." Listen to these words from **Jonathan Davis,** columnist for London's *The Spectator:* "Nothing highlights better the continuing gap between rhetoric and substance in British financial services than the failure of providers here to emulate Jack Bogle's index fund success in the United States. Every professional in the City knows that index funds should be core building blocks in any long-term investor's portfolio. Since 1976, the Vanguard index fund has produced a compound annual return of 12 percent, better than three-quarters of its peer group. Yet even 30 years on, ignorance and professional omerta still stand in the way of more investors enjoying the fruits of this unsung hero of the investment world."

Chapter Four

How Most Investors Turn a Winner's Game into a Loser's Game

—— ❧ ——

"The Relentless Rules of Humble Arithmetic"

BEFORE WE TURN TO the success of indexing as an investment strategy, let's explore in a bit more depth just why it is that investors as a group fail to earn the returns that our corporations generate through their dividends and earnings growth, ultimately reflected in the prices of their stocks. To understand why they do not, we need only to recognize the simple mathematics of investing: All investors as a group must necessarily earn precisely the market return, *but only before the costs of investing are deducted.*

After subtracting the costs of financial intermediation—all those management fees, all those brokerage commissions, all those sales loads, all those advertising costs, all those operating costs—the returns of investors as a group must, and will, and do fall short of the market return by an amount precisely equal to the aggregate amount of those costs. In a market that returns 10 percent, we investors together earn a gross return of 10 percent. (Duh!) But after we pay our financial intermediaries, we pocket only what remains. (And we pay them whether our returns are positive or negative!)

There are, then, these two certainties: (1) *Beating the market before costs is a zero-sum game*; (2) *Beating the market after costs is a loser's game.* The returns earned by investors in the aggregate inevitably fall well short of the returns that are realized in our financial markets. How much do those costs come to? For individual investors holding stocks directly, trading costs average about 1.5 percent per year. That cost is lower (about 1 percent) for those who trade infrequently, and much higher for investors who trade frequently (for example, 3 percent for investors who turn their portfolios over at a rate above 200 percent per year).

In equity mutual funds, management fees and operating expenses—combined, called the *expense ratio*—average about 1.5 percent per year of fund assets. Then add, say, another 0.5 percent in sales charges, assuming that a 5 percent initial sales charge is spread over a 10-year holding period. If the shares are held for five years, the cost would be twice that figure—1 percent per year.

But then add a giant additional cost, all the more pernicious by being invisible. I am referring to the hidden cost of portfolio turnover, estimated at a full 1 percent per year. The average fund turns its portfolio over at a rate of about 100 percent per year, meaning that a $5 billion fund buys $5 billion of stocks each year and sells another $5 billion. At that rate, brokerage commissions, bid-ask spreads, and market impact costs add a major layer of additional costs.

———————————— ⌇ ————————————

We investors as a group get precisely what we don't pay for. So if we pay nothing, we get everything.

———————————————————————

Result: the "all-in" cost of equity fund ownership can come to as much as 3 percent to 3.5 percent per year.* So yes, *costs matter*. The grim irony of investing, then, is that we investors as a group not only don't get what we pay for. We get precisely what we *don't* pay for. *So if we pay nothing, we get everything*. It's only common sense.

---

* I've ignored the hidden opportunity cost that fund investors pay. Most equity funds hold about 5 percent in cash reserves. If stocks earn a 10 percent return and these reserves earn 4 percent, that cost would add another 0.30 percent to the annual cost (5 percent multiplied by the 6 percent differential in earnings).

A few years ago when I was rereading *Other People's Money*, by Louis D. Brandeis (first published in 1914), I came across a wonderful passage that illustrates this simple lesson. Brandeis, later to become one of the most influential jurists in the history of the U.S. Supreme Court, railed against the oligarchs who a century ago controlled investment America and corporate America alike.

Brandeis described their self-serving financial management and their interlocking interests as, "trampling with impunity on laws human and divine, obsessed with the delusion that two plus two make five." He predicted (accurately, as it turned out) that the widespread speculation of that era would collapse, "*a victim of the relentless rules of humble arithmetic.*" He then added this unattributed warning—I'm guessing it's from Sophocles—"*Remember, O Stranger, arithmetic is the first of the sciences, and the mother of safety.*"

Brandeis's words hit me like the proverbial ton of bricks. Why? Because the relentless rules of the arithmetic of investing are so obvious. (It's been said by my detractors that all I have going for me is "the uncanny ability to recognize the obvious.") The curious fact is that most investors seem to have difficulty recognizing what lies in plain sight, right before their eyes. Or, perhaps even more pervasively, they refuse to recognize the reality because it flies in the face of their deep-seated beliefs, biases, overconfidence, and uncritical acceptance of the way that financial markets have worked, seemingly forever.

It's amazing how difficult it is for a man to understand something if he's paid a small fortune not to understand it.

What is more, it is hardly in the interest of our financial intermediaries to encourage their investor/clients to recognize the obvious reality. Indeed, the self-interest of the leaders of our financial system almost compels them to ignore these relentless rules. Paraphrasing Upton Sinclair: It's amazing how difficult it is for a man to understand something if he's paid a small fortune *not* to understand it.

Our system of financial intermediation has created enormous fortunes for those in the field of managing other people's money. Their self-interest will not soon change. But as an investor, you must look after your self-interest. Only by facing the obvious realities of investing can the intelligent investor succeed.

How much do the costs of financial intermediation matter? Hugely! In fact, the higher costs of equity funds have played the determinative role in explaining why fund managers have lagged the returns of the stock market so consistently, for so long. When you think about it, how could it be otherwise? By and large, these managers are smart, well-educated, experienced, knowledgeable, and honest. *But they are competing with each other*. When one buys a stock, another sells it. There is no net gain to fund shareholders as a group. In fact, they incur a loss equal to the transaction costs they pay to those Helpers that Warren Buffett warned us about in Chapter 1.

Investors pay far too little attention to the costs of investing. It's especially easy to underrate their importance under today's three conditions: (1) when so many costs are hidden from view (portfolio transaction costs, the unrecognized impact of front-end sales changes, taxes incurred on realized gains); (2) when stock market returns have been high (during the 1980s and 1990s, stock returns averaged 17.5 percent per year, and the average fund provided a nontrivial—but clearly inadequate—return of 15 percent); and especially (3) when investors focus on short-term returns, ignoring the truly confiscatory impact of cost over an investment lifetime.

Perhaps an example will help. Let's assume the stock market generates a total return averaging 8 percent per year over a half century. Yes, that's a long time, but an investment lifetime is now actually even longer—65 or 70 years for an investor who goes to work at age 22, begins to invest immediately, and works until, say, age 65; and then continues to invest over an actuarial expectancy of 20 or more years thereafter. Now let's assume that the costs of the average mutual fund continue at their present rate of at least 2.5 percent per year. Result: a *net* annual return of just 5.5 percent for the average fund.

$10,000 grows to $469,000 . . . or $145,400. Where did that $323,600 go?

Based on these assumptions, let's look at the returns earned on $10,000 over 50 years (Exhibit 4.1). The simple investment in the stock market grows to $469,000, a remarkable illustration of the magic of compounding returns over an investment lifetime. In the early years, the line showing the growth at a 5.5 percent annual rate doesn't look all that different from the growth in the stock market itself. But ever so slowly, the lines begin to diverge, finally at a truly dramatic rate. By the end of the long period, the value accumulated in the fund totals just $145,400, an astounding shortfall of $323,600 to the cumulative return earned in the market itself.

In the investment field, time doesn't heal all wounds. It makes them worse. *Where returns are concerned, time is your friend. But where costs are concerned, time*

Exhibit 4.1   The Magic of Compounding Returns, the Tyranny of Compounding Costs: Growth of $10,000 over 50 Years

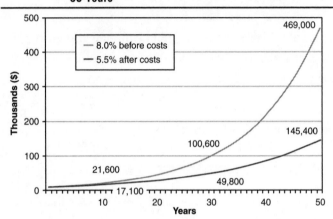

is your enemy. This point is powerfully illustrated when we consider how much of the value of the $10,000 investment is eroded with each passing year (Exhibit 4.2). By the end of the first year, only about 2 percent of the value of your capital has vanished ($10,800 vs. $10,550). By the 10th year, 21 percent has vanished ($21,600 vs. $17,100). By the 30th year, 50 percent has vanished ($100,600 vs. $49,800). And by the end of the investment period, costs have consumed nearly 70 percent of the potential accumulation available simply by holding the market portfolio.

Exhibit 4.2   The Tyranny of Compounding: Long-Term Impact of Lagging the Market by 2.5 Percent

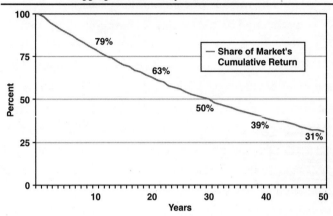

The investor, who put up 100 percent of the capital and assumed 100 percent of the risk, earned only 31 percent of the market return. The system of financial intermediation, which put up zero percent of the capital and assumed zero percent of the risk, essentially confiscated 70 percent of that return—surely the lion's share. What you see here—and please don't ever forget it!—is that over the long term, the miracle of compounding *returns* is overwhelmed by the tyranny of compounding *costs*. Add that mathematical certainty to the relentless rules of humble arithmetic described earlier.

---------------- ∼ ----------------

**The miracle of compounding returns is
overwhelmed by the tyranny of compounding costs.**

But enough of theory and hypothetical examples. Let's
see how this principle works in the real world. During the
quarter century from 1980 to 2005, the return on the stock
market (measured by the Standard & Poor's 500 Index) averaged 12.5 percent per year. The return on the average mutual fund averaged just 10.0 percent. That 2.5 percent
differential is about what one might have expected, given our
earlier 3 percent rough estimate of fund costs. (Never forget:
Market return, minus cost, equals investor return.) Simply
put, our fund managers, sitting at the top of the investment
food chain, have confiscated an excessive share of the financial markets' returns. Fund investors, inevitably at the bottom of the food chain, have been left with too small a share.

Investors need not have incurred that loss. For they
could have easily invested in a simple index fund tracking
the S&P 500. Such a fund actually returned 12.3 percent
per year during that period—the market return of 12.5 percent less costs of just 0.2 percent. That is an annual margin
of superiority of 2.3 percent over the average fund.

On first impression, that annual gap may not look
large. But when compounded over 25 years, it reaches
staggering proportions. A $10,000 initial investment in the

index fund grew by a remarkable $170,800, compared with growth of just $98,200 in the average equity mutual fund— only 57 percent of the total accumulation in the index fund.

But let's face the facts. Both of these accumulations are overstated because they are based on 2005 dollars, which have less than half the spending power they enjoyed in 1980. During this period, inflation eroded the real buying power of these returns at an average rate of 3.3 percent per year. When we turn those nominal dollars—the dollars that we earn and spend and invest every day—into real dollars that are adjusted to take inflation into account, the results for that original $10,000 investment tumble sharply. The cumulative real profit, after compounding, came to just $40,600 for the average actively managed equity fund, compared with $76,200 for the passively managed index fund (Exhibit 4.3).

Now, the average fund produced barely one-half (actually 53 percent) of the profit earned by the stock market through the simple index fund—a return that was there for the taking. (It is in the nature of arithmetic that deducting the same inflation rate from both figures further increases the comparative advantage of the investment with the higher return, in this case the index fund.) Yes, *costs matter!* Indeed, costs make the difference between investment success and investment failure.

In short, the humble arithmetic of investing—the logical, inevitable, and unyielding penalty assessed by investment costs

**EXHIBIT 4.3   Index Fund versus Managed Fund:
Profit on Initial Investment of $10,000, 1980–2005**

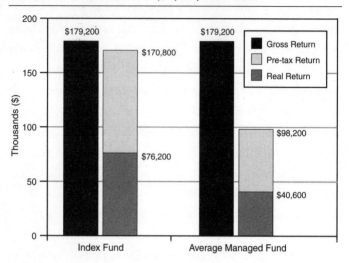

Note: Assumes reinvestment of all dividends and capital gains.

and rising living costs—has devastated the returns earned by
mutual fund investors. Using Justice Brandeis's formulation,
our mutual fund managers seem obsessed with the delusion—
and are foisting that delusion on investors—that a *nominal
gross* return of 12.5 percent per year in the stock market,
minus fund expenses of 2.5 percent, minus inflation of 3.3
percent, still equals a *real net* return of 12.5 percent. Well, to
state the obvious, it doesn't. You can add and subtract for
yourself. It equals (you guessed it) only 6.7 percent.

Unless the fund industry changes and improves the net return it delivers to fund shareholders, it will falter and finally fail, a victim, yes, of the relentless rules of humble arithmetic. Were he looking over your shoulder as you read this book, Justice Brandeis surely would be warning you, *"Remember, O reader, that arithmetic is the first of the sciences and the mother of safety."*

So, sharpen your pencils. Do your own arithmetic. Realize that you are not consigned to playing the hyperactive management game that is played by the overwhelming majority of individual investors and mutual fund owners alike. The index fund is there to guarantee that you will earn your fair share of whatever returns our businesses earn and our stock market delivers.

Don't Take My Word for It

The innate superiority of the index fund has been endorsed (perhaps grudgingly) by a wide range of mutual fund industry insiders. When he retired, here's what **Peter Lynch**, the legendary manager who steered Fidelity Magellan Fund to such great success during his 1977 to 1990 tenure, had to say in *Barron's:* "The S&P is up 343.8 percent for 10 years. That is a four-bagger. The general equity funds are up 283 percent. So it's getting worse, the

(continued)

deterioration by professionals is getting worse. *The public would be better off in an index fund."* Now hear industry leader **Jon Fossel,** former chairman of The Investment Company Institute and of the Oppenheimer Funds in the *Wall Street Journal:* "People ought to recognize that the average fund can *never* outperform the market in total." (Italics added.)

Even hyperactive investors seem to believe in indexing strategies. Here's what **James J. Cramer,** money manager and host of CNBC's *Mad Money* says: "After a lifetime of picking stocks, I have to admit that Bogle's arguments in favor of the index fund have me thinking of joining him rather than trying to beat him. Bogle's wisdom and common sense [are] indispensable . . . for anyone trying to figure out how to invest in this crazy stock market." And hedge fund managers, too, join the chorus. One of money management's giants, **Clifford A. Asness,** managing and founding principal of AQR Capital Management, adds his own wisdom, expertise, and integrity: "Market-cap based indexing will never be driven from its deserved perch as core and deserved king of the investment world. It is what we should all own in theory and it has delivered low-cost equity returns to a great mass of investors . . . the now and forever king-of-the-hill."

Chapter Five

The Grand Illusion

— ⌁ —

Surprise! The Returns Reported by Mutual Funds Aren't Actually Earned by Mutual Fund Investors.

IT IS GRATIFYING THAT industry insiders such as the Investment Company Institute's (ICI's) chairman Jon Fossel, Fidelity's Peter Lynch, *Mad Money's* James Cramer, and AQR's Clifford Asness agree with me about the inevitable inadequacy of returns earned by the typical equity mutual fund relative to the returns available simply by owning the stock market through an index fund based on the S&P 500. But the idea that fund investors *themselves* actually earn those returns proves to be a grand illusion. Not only an illusion, but a generous one. The reality is considerably worse. For in addition to paying the heavy costs that fund managers extract for their services, the shareholders pay an additional cost that has been even larger.

During the 25-year period examined in Chapter 4, the returns we presented were based on the traditional *time-weighted* returns reported by the funds—the change in the asset value of each fund share, adjusted to reflect the reinvestment of all income dividends and capital gains distributions. But that *fund* return does not tell us what return was earned by the average fund investor. And that return turns out to be far lower.

~

Hint: money flows into most funds after good performance, and goes out when bad performance follows.

To ascertain the return earned by the average fund investor, we must consider the *dollar-weighted* return, which accounts for the impact of capital flows from investors, into and out of the fund.* (Hint: money flows into most funds after good performance is achieved, and goes out when bad performance follows.)

When we compare traditionally calculated fund returns with the returns actually earned by their investors

---

* If a $100 million fund earns a return of 30 percent during a given year and $1 billion of its shares are purchased on the final day of the year, the average return earned by its investors would be just 4.9 percent.

over the past quarter century, it turns out that the average fund investor earned, not the 10.0 percent reported by the average fund, but 7.3 percent—an annual return fully 2.7 percentage points per year less than that of the fund. (In fairness, the index fund investor, too, was enticed by the rising market, and earned a return of 10.8 percent, 1.5 percentage points short of the fund return itself.)

Yes, during the past 25 years, while the stock market index fund was providing an annual return of 12.3 percent and the average equity *fund* was earning an annual return of 10.0 percent, the average fund *investor* was earning only 7.3 percent a year.

Compounded over the full period, as we saw in Chapter 4, the 2.5 percent penalty incurred by the average fund because of costs was huge. But the dual penalties of faulty timing and adverse selection were even larger. Exhibit 5.1 shows that $10,000 invested in the index fund grew to $170,800; in the average equity fund, to $98,200—just 57 percent of what was there for the taking. But the compound return earned by the average fund investor tumbled to $48,200, a stunning 28 percent of the return on the simple index fund.

And once again, the value of all those dollars tumbles because we must take inflation into account. The index fund real return drops to 9.0 percent per year, but the real return of the average fund investor plummets to just 4.0 percent. On a compounded basis, $76,200 of real

**EXHIBIT 5.1 Index Fund versus Managed Fund:
Profit on Initial Investment of $10,000, 1980–2005**

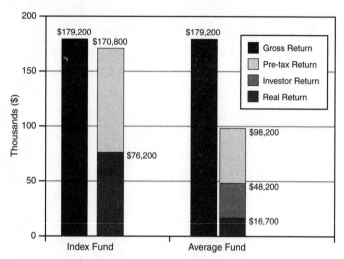

Note: Assumes reinvestment of all dividends and capital gains.

value for the index fund versus just $16,700 for the fund investor—only 22 percent of the potential accumulation that was there for the taking. Truth told, it's hard to imagine such a staggering gap, but facts are facts.

While the data clearly indicate that fund investor returns fell well short of fund returns, there is no way to be precise about the exact shortfall.* But the point of this examination of the returns earned by the stock market, the average fund,

* Estimate of the gap was based on the difference between the 10-year time-weighted returns on the 200 largest mutual funds in 1999 and their actual dollar-weighted returns during the same period.

and the average fund owner is not precision, but direction. Whatever the precise data, the evidence is compelling that equity fund returns lag the stock market by a substantial amount, largely accounted for by their costs, and that fund investor returns lag fund returns by an even larger amount.

~

Inflamed by heady optimism and greed, and enticed by the wiles of mutual fund marketers, investors poured their savings into equity funds at the bull market peak.

What explains this shocking lag? Simply put, counter-productive market timing and fund selection. First, shareholders investing in equity funds paid a heavy timing penalty. They invested too little of their savings in equity funds during the 1980s and early 1990s when stocks represented good values. Then, inflamed by the heady optimism and greed of the era and enticed by the wiles of mutual fund marketers as the bull market neared its peak, they poured too much of their savings into equity funds. Second, they paid a selection penalty, pouring their money into the market not only at the wrong time but into the wrong funds. In both failures, investors simply failed to practice what common sense would have told them.

This lag effect was amazingly pervasive. In the past decade, the returns provided to investors by 198 of the

200 most popular equity funds of 1996 to 2000 were lower than the returns that they reported to investors! This lag was especially evident during the "new economy" craze of the late 1990s. Then, the fund industry organized more and more funds, usually funds that carried considerably higher risk than the stock market itself, and magnified the problem by heavily advertising the eye-catching past returns earned by its hottest funds.

As the market soared, investors poured ever larger sums of money into equity funds. They invested a net total of only $18 billion in 1990 when stocks were cheap, but $420 billion in 1999 and 2000, when stocks were overvalued (Exhibit 5.2). What's more, they also chose overwhelmingly the highest-risk growth funds, to the virtual exclusion of more conservative value-oriented funds. While only 20 percent of their money went into risky aggressive growth funds in 1990, they poured fully 95 percent into such funds when they peaked during 1999 and early 2000. After the fall, when it was too late, investor purchases dried up to as little as $50 billion in 2002, when the market hit bottom. They also pulled their money out of growth funds and turned, too late, to value funds.

The problems of counterproductive market timing and unwise fund selection can be illustrated by observing the experience of the most popular growth funds of five giant fund families with the largest cash inflows, altogether more

EXHIBIT 5.2   The Timing and Selection Penalties: Net Flow into Equity Funds

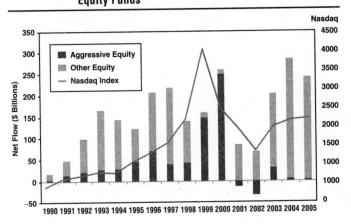

than $150 billion between 1996 and 2000 inclusive (Exhibit 5.3). During those five years, these aggressive funds provided spectacular records—annual returns averaging 21 percent per year, well above even the outstanding return of 18.4 percent on the S&P 500 Index fund. But during the five years that followed, in 2001 through 2005, retribution followed. While the index fund eked out a small gain (less than 1 percent per year), the returns of these aggressive, risk-laden funds tumbled into negative territory.

For the full 10 years, taking into account both their rise and their fall, the returns reported by these aggressive funds were actually quite acceptable—an average of 7.8

EXHIBIT 5.3 Growth Fund Returns versus Investor Returns: Aggressive Growth Funds, 1995–2005

Fund Group Overall Manager	1995–2000 Total	2000–2005 Total	Annual Return 10-Year Fund	10-Year Shareholder	10-Year Shareholder Lag
Alliance Bernstein Growth	20.1%	−5.2%	6.7%	−7.6%	−14.3%
Fidelity Growth	21.6	−2.5	8.8	3.4	−5.5
Janus Growth	24.8	−3.3	9.8	1.4	−8.5
MFS Growth	20.7	−4.6	7.3	−1.1	−8.4
Putnam Growth	17.6	−3.7	6.5	1.7	−4.8
Average	21.0%	−3.9%	7.8%	−0.5%	−8.3%
Vanguard Index 500	18.4%	0.5%	9.1%	7.1%	−2.0%

percent per year, nearly equal to the return of 9.1 percent for the index fund. But woe to the shareholder who chose them. For while the fund returns were acceptable, the returns of their shareholders were, well, terrible.

Their average return came to minus 0.4 percent per year, in negative territory and a lag of fully 8.3 percentage points behind the funds' reported per share figure. For the record, the annual return of the index fund shareholder, at 7.1 percent, also lagged the return of the fund, but by only 2.0 percentage points, far less than this group's gap of 8.3 percentage points, or even the industry gap of 2.7 percentage points.

When the annual returns of these aggressive funds are compounded over the full period, the deterioration is stunning: a cumulative fund return averaging more than 112 percent; a cumulative shareholder return averaging negative 4.5 percent. That's a lag of more than 117 percentage points! This astonishing penalty, then, makes clear the perils of fund selection and timing. It also illustrates the value of indexing and the necessity of setting a sound course and then sticking to it, come what may.

— ∿ —

When ever-counterproductive investor emotions are played on by ever-counterproductive fund industry promotions, little good is apt to result.

The shocking performance of fund investors during the stock market "new economy" bubble is unusual in its dimension, but not in its existence. Fund investors have been chasing past performance since time eternal, allowing their emotions—perhaps even their greed—to overwhelm their reason. But the fund industry itself has played on these emotions, bringing out new funds to meet the fads and fashions of the day, often supercharged and speculative, and then aggressively advertising and marketing them. It is fair to say that when ever-counterproductive investor emotions are played on by ever-counterproductive fund industry promotions, little good is apt to result.

The fund industry will not soon give up its promotions. But the intelligent investor will be well advised to heed not only the message in Chapter 4 about minimizing expenses, but the message in this chapter about getting emotions out of the equation. The beauty of the index fund, then, lies not only in its low expenses, but in its elimination of all those tempting fund choices that promise so much and deliver so little. Unlike the hot funds of the day, the index fund can be held through thick and thin for an investment lifetime, and emotions need never enter the equation. The winning formula for success in investing is owning the entire stock market through an index fund, and then doing nothing. Just stay the course.

Don't Take My Word for It

The wise **Warren Buffett** shares my view, in what I call his *"four E's."* "The greatest Enemies of the Equity investor are Expenses and Emotions." Even **Andrew Lo,** MIT professor and author of *A Non-Random Walk Down Wall Street* (suggesting strategies to outperform the market), personally "invests by buying and holding index funds." Perhaps even more surprisingly, the founder and chief executive of the largest mutual supermarket—while vigorously promoting actively managed funds—favors the classic index fund for himself. When asked why people invest in managed funds, **Charles Schwab** answered: "It's fun to play around. . . it's human nature to try to select the right horse . . . (But) for the average person, I'm more of an indexer. . . The predictability is so high . . . For 10, 15, 20 years you'll be in the 85th percentile of performance. Why would you screw it up?"

Mark Hulbert, highly regarded editor of the *Hulbert Financial Digest* concurs. "Assuming that the future is like the past, you can outperform 80 percent of your fellow investors over the next several decades by investing in an index fund—and doing nothing else. [But] acquire the discipline to do something even better: become a long-term index fund investor." His *New York Times* article was headlined: "Buy and Hold? Sure, but Don't Forget the Hold."

Chapter Six

Taxes Are Costs, Too

——— ∾ ———

Don't Pay Uncle Sam Any More Than You Should.

WE STILL AREN'T THROUGH with these relentless rules of humble arithmetic—the logical, inevitable, and unyielding long-term penalties assessed against stock market participants by investment expenses and the powerful impact of inflation—that have slashed the capital accumulated by mutual fund investors. As described in Chapter 4, the index fund has provided excellent protection from the penalty of these costs. While its real returns also were hurt by inflation, the cumulative impact was far less than on the actively managed equity funds.

But there is yet another cost—too often ignored—that slashes even further the net returns that investors actually receive. I'm referring to taxes—federal, state, and local income taxes.* And here again, the index fund garners a substantial edge. The fact is that most managed mutual funds are astonishingly tax-inefficient, a result of the short-term focus of their portfolio managers, usually frenetic traders of the stocks in the portfolios they supervise.

Managed mutual funds are astonishingly tax-inefficient.

The turnover of the average equity fund now comes to about 100 percent per year. (In fairness, based on total assets rather than number of funds, the turnover rate of actively managed funds is 61 percent.) Industrywide, the average stock is held by the average fund for an average of just 12 months. (Based on equity fund total assets, only 20 months.) Hard as it is to imagine, from 1945 to 1965, the turnover rate averaged just 16 percent per year, an average holding period of six years for the average stock in a fund portfolio. This huge increase in turnover and its attendant transaction costs have ill-served fund investors.

---

*About one-half of all equity mutual fund shares are held by individual investors in fully taxable investment accounts. The other half are held in tax-deferred accounts such as individual retirement accounts (IRAs) and corporate savings, thrift, and profit-sharing plans. If your fund holdings are solely in the latter category, you need not be concerned with the discussion in this chapter.

This pattern of tax-inefficiency for active managers seems destined to continue as long as (1) stocks rise, and (2) fund managers continue their hyperactive patterns of short-term trading. Let's be clear: Most fund managers, once focused on long-term investment, are now focused on short-term speculation. But the index fund follows precisely the opposite policy—buying and holding forever, and incurring transaction costs that are somewhere between infinitesimal and zero.

So let's pick up where we left off two chapters ago, with the net annual return of 10.0 percent for the average equity fund over the past 25 years can be compared with the 12.3 percent return for the S&P 500 Index fund. With the high portfolio turnover of actively managed funds, their taxable investors were subject to an estimated effective annual federal tax of 1.8 percentage points per year (state and local taxes would further balloon the figure), reducing the after-tax annual return to 8.2 percent (Exhibit 6.1).

Despite the higher returns that they earned, investors in the index fund were actually subjected to lower taxes—in fact, at 0.6 percentage points, only about one-third of that tax burden—bringing their after-tax return to 11.7 percent. Compounded, the initial $10,000 investment grew by just $61,700 after taxes for the active funds, nearly 60 percent less than

**EXHIBIT 6.1   Index Fund versus Managed Fund:
Profit on Initial Investment of $10,000, 1980–2005**

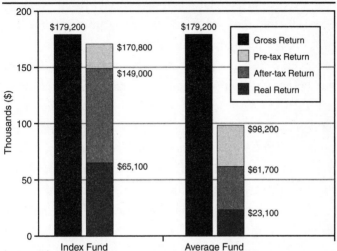

Note: Assumes reinvestment of all dividends and capital gains.

the $149,000 of accumulated growth in the index fund,
a loss of some $87,300.*

What's more, just as fund expenses are paid in current dollars, so is your annual tax bill. When we calculate
the accumulated wealth in terms of real dollars with 1980
buying power, investor wealth again contracts dramati-
cally. The annual real return of the average equity fund
now drops to 4.9 percent, less than 60 percent of the 8.4

---

*The index fund investor would be subject to taxes on any gains realized
when liquidating shares. But for an investor who bequeaths shares to heirs,
the cost would be "stepped up" to their market value on date of death and
no capital gain would be recognized or taxed.

percent actual return of the index fund. Compounded, the real after-tax accumulation on that initial $10,000 came to $65,100 for the index fund, nearly three *times* the $23,100 for the active equity index fund.

Even with the more subdued returns earned in the postbubble era, actively managed funds persist in foisting this extraordinarily costly tax inefficiency on their shareholders. While the net annual return of the average equity fund was 8.5 percent over the past decade (1996 to 2005), the tax bill consumed fully 1.7 percentage points of the return, reducing the net fund return to just 6.8 percent.

I hesitate to assign the responsibility for being "the straw that broke the camel's back" of equity fund returns to any single one of these negative factors. But surely the final straws include (1) high costs, (2) the adverse investor selections and counterproductive market timing described in Chapter 5, and (3) taxes. Whatever way one looks at it, the camel's back is surely broken. But the very last straw, it turns out, is inflation.

Fund returns are devastated by costs, taxes, and inflation.

When we pay our fund costs in *current* dollars, year after year—and that's exactly how we pay our fund expenses and our taxes on fund capital gains (often realized on a short-term basis, to boot)—and yet accumulate our assets only in *real* dollars, eroded by the relentless rise in the cost of living that seems imbedded in our economy, the results are devastating. It is truly remarkable—and hardly praiseworthy—that this devastation is virtually ignored in the information that fund managers provide to fund investors.

A paradox: While the index fund is remarkably tax-*efficient* in managing capital gains, it turns out to be relatively tax-*inefficient* in distributing dividend income. Why? Because its rock-bottom costs mean that nearly all the dividends paid on the stocks held by the low-cost index fund actually flow directly into the hands of the index fund's shareholders. With the high expense ratios incurred by managed funds, however, only a tiny portion of the dividends that the funds receive actually find their way into the hands of the fund's shareholders.

Here is the unsurprising and ever relentless arithmetic: the annual gross dividend yield earned by the typical active equity fund *before deducting fund expenses* is about the same as the dividend yield of the low-cost index fund—1.8 percent in late-2006. But after deducting the 1.5 percent of expenses borne by the typical active fund, its net dividend yield drops to just 0.3 percent (!) for its owners. Fund operating costs and fees confiscate fully 80 percent of its dividend income, a sad reaffirmation of the eternal position of fund investors at the bottom of the mutual fund food chain.

The expense ratio of a low-cost index fund is about 0.15 percent, consuming only 8 percent of its 1.8 percent dividend yield. The result: a net yield of 1.65 percent to distribute to the passively managed index fund owners, a dividend merely 5.5 times as high as the dividend yield of 0.3 percent on the actively managed fund.

For taxable shareholders, that larger dividend is subject to the current 15 percent federal tax on dividend income, consuming about 0.27 percentage points of the yield. Paradoxically, the active fund, with an effective tax rate of just 0.045 percent (15 percent of the 0.3 percent net yield), appears more tax efficient from a dividend standpoint. But the reality is that the tax imposed by the active managers in the form of the fees it deducts before paying those dividends has already consumed 80 percent of the yield. The wise investor will seek the dividend "tax-inefficiency" of the index fund dividend rather than the "tax-efficiency" of most actively managed funds engendered by their confiscatory operating costs.

Don't Take My Word for It

Consider these words from a paper by **John B. Shoven,** of Stanford University and the National Bureau of Economic Research, and **Joel M. Dickson,**

(continued)

then of the Federal Reserve System: "Mutual funds have failed to manage their realized capital gains in such a way as to permit a substantial deferral of taxes (raising) investors' tax bills considerably. . . . If the Vanguard 500 Index Fund could have deferred all of its realized capital gains, it would have ended up in the 91.8 percentile for the high tax investor" (i.e., it outpaced 92 percent of all managed equity funds).

Or listen to investment adviser **William Bernstein,** author of *The Four Pillars of Investing:* "While it is probably a poor idea to own actively managed mutual funds in general, it is truly a *terrible* idea to own them in taxable accounts . . . (taxes are) a drag on performance of up to 4 percentage points each year . . . many index funds allow your capital gains to grow largely undisturbed until you sell. . . . *For the taxable investor, indexing means never having to say you're sorry.*"

And **Dr. Malkiel** again casts his lot with the index fund: "Index funds are . . . tax friendly, allowing investors to defer the realization of capital gains or avoid them completely if the shares are later bequeathed. To the extent that the long-run uptrend in stock prices continues, switching from security to security involves realizing capital gains that are subject to tax. Taxes are a crucially important financial consideration because the earlier realization of capital gains will substantially reduce net returns. Index funds do not trade from security to security and, thus, they tend to avoid capital gains taxes."

Chapter Seven

When the Good Times No Longer Roll

What Happens If Future Returns Are Lower?

REMEMBER THE UNFAILING principle described in Chapter 2: in the long run it is the reality of business—the dividend yields and earnings growth of corporations—that drives the returns generated by the stock market. However, I must warn you that during the past 25 years—the period examined in the three preceding chapters—the 12.5 percent nominal annual return provided by the U.S. stock market included a speculative return of nearly 3 percent per year, far above the business reality.

Recall that the century-plus nominal investment return earned by stocks was 9.5 percent, consisting of an average dividend yield of 4.5 percent and average annual earnings growth of 5.0 percent. A mere 0.1 percent per year—what I described as speculative return—was added by the rise in the price/earnings ratio from 15 times at the beginning of the period to 18 times at its end, bringing the *total* annual return to 9.6 percent.*

Paradoxically, the *investment* return earned by stocks over the past 25 years was hardly extraordinary. A dividend yield averaging 3.4 percent plus annual earnings growth of 6.4 percent brought it to 9.8 percent, almost precisely equal to the historical norm of 9.5 percent. But, illustrating the difficulty of forecasting changes in the amount that investors are willing to pay for each dollar of corporate earnings, the speculative return was anything but normal.

Common sense tells us that we're facing an era of subdued returns in the stock market.

As investor confidence rose, so did the price/earnings (P/E) ratio rise—from 9 times to 18 times, an amazing 100

---

* A more-than-technical caveat: due to the issuance of additional shares of stock by corporations over the years, the rate of growth of corporate earnings per share is estimated to lag the growth of aggregate corporate earnings by as much as 2 percentage points per year.

percent increase, adding fully 2.7 percentage points per year—almost 30 percent—to the solid 9.8 percent fundamental return. (Early in 2000, the P/E ratio had actually risen to an astonishing 32 times, only to plummet to 18 times as the new economy bubble burst.) Result: speculative return was responsible for more than 20 percent of the market's 12.5 percent annual return during this period. Since it is unrealistic to expect the P/E ratio to double in the coming decade, a similar 12.5 percent return is unlikely to recur. Common sense tells us that we're facing an era of subdued returns in the stock market (Exhibit 7.1).

EXHIBIT 7.1   Total Returns on Stocks, Past and Future

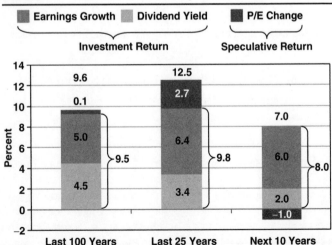

Why? First, because today's dividend yield on stocks is not 4.5 percent (the historical rate), but slightly below 2 percent. Thus we can expect a dead-weight loss of 2.5 percentage points per year in the contribution of dividend income to investment return. Let's assume that corporate earnings will continue (as, over time, they usually have) to grow at about the pace of our economy's expected nominal growth rate of 5 or 6 percent per year over the coming decade. If that's correct, then the most likely investment return on stocks would be in the range of 7 to 8 percent. I'll be optimistic and project an annual investment return (a bit nervously!) averaging 8 percent.

Second, the present price/earnings multiple on stocks looks to be about 18 times based on the trailing 12-month *reported* earnings of the S&P 500 (16 times if we use projected *operating* earnings, which exclude write-offs for discontinued business activities). If it remains at that level a decade hence, speculative return would neither add to nor detract from that possible 8 percent investment return. My guess (it is little more than that) is that the P/E might ease down to, say, 16 times, reducing the market's return by about 1 percentage point a year, to an annual rate of 7 percent. You don't have to agree with me. If you think it will leap to 25 times, *add* 3 percentage points, bringing the total return on stocks to 11 percent. If you think it will drop to

12 times, *subtract* 4 percentage points; reducing the total return on stocks to 4 percent.

------------------------------ ∼ ------------------------------

If rational expectations suggest future annual returns of about 7 percent on stocks, what does this imply for returns on equity funds?

Now assume that 7 percent is a rational expectation for future stock market returns. To calculate the return for the average actively managed equity mutual fund in such an environment, simply remember the humble arithmetic of fund investing: nominal market return, minus investment costs, minus taxes (reduced to reflect lower capital gains realization), minus an assumed inflation rate of 2.3 percent (the rate the financial markets are now expecting over the coming decade) equals just 1.4 percent per year (Exhibit 7.2). I simply didn't have the courage to make another deduction to reflect the impact of the counterproductive timing and adverse fund selection that will likely continue to bedevil the typical fund shareholder. It may seem absurd to project such a low return for the typical equity fund investor. *But the numbers are there*. Again, feel free to disagree and to project the future using your own rational expectations.

In summary, the future outlook for stock returns is far below the long-term real return on U.S. stocks of

EXHIBIT 7.2   Index Fund versus Managed Fund: Projected Profit on Initial Investment of $10,000, 2006–2016

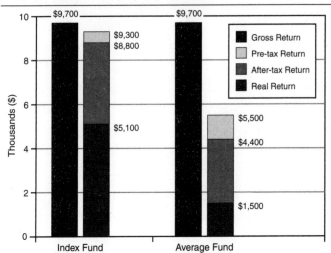

Note: Assumes reinvestment of all dividends and capital gains.

about 6.5 percent annually. My projection of a future real return of 4.7 percent (before costs and taxes) is conservative largely because today's dividend yield of 2 percent is below the long-term norm of 4.5 percent, partially offset by my optimistic projection of real earnings growth of 2.5 percent per year versus the 1.5 percent long-term norm. The real long-term rate of per share earnings growth of U.S. corporations has been no more than that humble figure. As suggested earlier, some experts put the figure at only 1 percent on an earnings per share basis.

In any event, in a likely future environment of lower returns on equities, the low-cost, tax-efficient index fund would provide even higher real returns relative to actively managed equity funds than the enormous advantage it has achieved over the past quarter century. Yes, a real 10-year gain of $5,100 on a $10,000 investment in the index fund is nothing to write home about. But what's to be said about the mere $1,500 profit that could well be what the typical managed equity fund delivers?

Unless the fund industry begins to change, the typical actively managed fund appears to be a singularly unfortunate investment choice.

The fact is that lower returns harshly magnify the relentless arithmetic of excessive mutual fund costs, even ignoring all those unnecessary taxes. Why? While costs of 2.5 percentage points would consume "only" 16 percent of a 15 percent return and "only" 25 percent of a 10 percent return, such costs would consume nearly 40 percent of a 7 percent *nominal* return and (I hope you're sitting down) nearly 60 percent of the 4.5 real return on stocks that rational expectations suggest. Unless the fund industry begins to change—by reducing management fees, operating expenses, sales charges, and portfolio turnover, with its attendant costs—the typical actively managed fund appears to be a singularly unfortunate choice for investors.

The 1.2 percent expected annual real return that the average equity fund might deliver is unacceptable. What can equity fund investors do to avoid being trapped by these relentless rules of arithmetic, so devastating when applied to future returns that are likely to be well below long-term norms? There are at least five options for improving on it: (1) Select winning funds on the basis of their long-term past records. (2) Select winning funds on the basis of their recent short-term performance. (3) Get some professional advice in selecting funds that are likely to outpace the market. (4) Select funds with rock-bottom costs, minimal portfolio turnover, and no sales loads. Or (5) Select a low-cost index fund that simply holds the stock market portfolio.

In Chapters 8 through 12, we'll examine each of these options.

Don't Take My Word for It

Financial advisers seem to agree with my appraisal of future returns. In the latter part of 2006, in a speech before these professionals at their Chicago convention, I polled the audience. The clear consensus: stock returns of 6.5 percent over the coming decade.

(continued)

Investment bankers are of a similar mind. When **Henry McVey,** market strategist for Morgan Stanley, polled the chief financial officers of the 100 largest corporations in the United States, they expected a future return on stocks of 6.6 percent. (One wonders how these executives can justify their implicit assumption that the stocks in their companies' pension plans will return 11 percent per year.)

Other highly regarded investment strategists also share my general view that we are facing a new era of subdued investment returns. **Gary P. Brinson,** CFA, former president of UBS Investment Management, is one whose assessment about future returns echoes my own. "Today's investment market fundamentals and financial variables clearly suggest that future real returns from a mixed portfolio of stocks, bonds, and other assets (such as real estate) are unlikely to be greater than 4.5 to 5.0 percent. With an inflation assumption of 2.5 percent, nominal returns greater than 7.0 to 7.5 percent for these portfolios are unrealistic. What cannot be explained is why people are willing to pay the considerable fees (involved). Perhaps they are paying for historical returns, for hope, or out of desperation... "For the markets in total, the amount of value added, or alpha, must sum to zero. One person's positive alpha is someone else's negative alpha. Collectively, for the institutional, mutual fund, and private banking arenas, the aggregate alpha return will be zero or negative after transaction costs. Aggregate fees for the active managers should thus be, at most, the fees associated with passive management. Yet, these fees are several times larger than fees that would be associated with passive management. This illogical conundrum will ultimately have to end."

Or consider these words by **Richard M. Ennis,** CFA, Ennis Knupp + Associates, and editor of the *Financial Analysts Journal:* "Today, with interest rates near 4 percent and stocks yielding less than 2 percent, few among us expect double-digit investment returns for any extended period in the near future. Yet, we live with a legacy of that era: historically high fee structures brought on by trillions upon trillions of dollars seeking growth during the boom and shelter in its aftermath. Second, facing the dual challenge of market efficiency and high costs, investors will continue to shift assets from active to passive management. And third, some of active management's true believers will shift assets from expensive products to more reasonably priced products. Impetus for this move will be the growing realization that high fees sap the performance potential of even skillful managers."

Chapter Eight

Selecting Long-Term Winners

~

Don't Look for the Needle—
Buy the Haystack.

SELECTING WINNING FUNDS in advance is more difficult than it looks. Sure, there are always some winners
that survive over the years. And if we pore over records
of past performance, it is easy to find them. The mutual
funds we hear the most about are those that have lit up
the skies with their glow of past success. We don't hear
much about those that did well for a while—even for a
long while—and then faltered. And when they falter, they
often go out of business, consigned to the dustbin of mutual fund history. But easy as it is to identify past winners,

there is little evidence that such performance persists in the future.

Let's begin by considering the records of funds that have won over the long term. Exhibit 8.1 goes back to 1970 and shows the 36-year records of the 355 equity funds that existed at the start of that period. The first and most obvious surprise awaits you: fully 223 of those funds—almost two-thirds—have gone out of business. If your fund doesn't last for the long term, how can you invest for the long term?

You can safely assume it was not the best performers that have gone to their well-earned demise; it was the laggards that disappeared. Sometimes their managers

EXHIBIT 8.1   Winners, Losers, and Failures: Long-Term Returns of Mutual Funds, 1970–2005

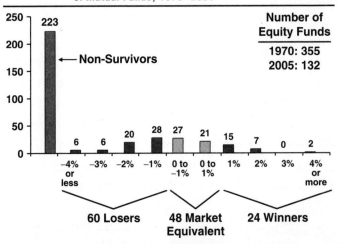

moved on. (The average fund portfolio manager, in fact, lasts just five years.) Sometimes giant financial conglomerates acquired their management companies, and the new owners decided to "clean up the product line." (These conglomerates, truth told, are in business primarily to earn a return on *their* capital, not on the fund investor's capital.) Funds with lagging performance saw their investors flee, and they became a drag on their managers' profits. There are many reasons that funds disappear, few of them good.

A death in the family.

Even funds with solid long-term records go out of business. Often, their management companies are acquired by marketing companies whose ambitious executives conclude that, however good the funds' early records, they are not exciting enough to draw huge amounts of capital from new investors. The funds have simply outlived their usefulness. In other cases, a few years of faltering performance does the job. Sadly, the second oldest fund in the entire mutual fund industry was a recent victim of these attitudes, put out of business by a new owner of its management company. After surviving all the tempestuous markets of the past 80 years: *State Street Investment Trust, 1925–2005, R.I.P.* As one of the longest-serving participants in the fund industry, who clearly remembers the classy record of this fund over so many years, I regard the loss of State Street as a death in the family.

In any event, 223 of the equity funds of 1970 are gone, mostly the poor performers. Another 60 remain, yet significantly underperformed the S&P 500 by more than 1 percentage point per year. Together, then, 283 funds—nearly 80 percent of the funds among those original 355—have, one way or another, failed to distinguish themselves. Another 48 funds provided returns within one percentage point, plus or minus, of the return of the S&P 500—market-matchers, as it were.

That leaves just 24 mutual funds—*only one out of every 14*—that outpaced the market by more than one percentage point per year. Let's face it: those are terrible odds! What's more, the margin of superiority of 15 of those 24 funds over the S&P 500 was less than 2 percentage points per year, a superiority that may be due as much to luck as to skill.

That still leaves us with nine solid long-term winners. It is a tremendous accomplishment to outpace the market by 2 percentage points or more of annual return over 35 years. Make no mistake about that. But, here a curious— perhaps almost obvious—fact emerges (Exhibit 8.2). Six of those nine winners achieved their superiority many years ago, often when they were of small size.

Exhibit 8.2   Now, About Those Nine Winners

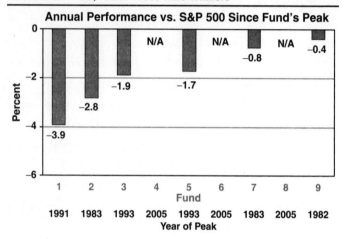

When the accomplishments of these nine successful mutual funds were noticed by investors, cash poured in, and they got large. But, as Warren Buffett reminds us, "a fat wallet is the enemy of superior returns." And so it was. As they grew, the records of six of them turned lackluster. One fund reached its performance peak way back in 1982, 24 long years ago. On balance, it has lagged ever since. Two others peaked in 1983. The remaining three peaked no more recently than 1993, more than a decade ago. (One of these was Peter Lynch's legendary Fidelity Magellan Fund, which has now been struggling for 13 years.)

That leaves just three funds. Only three out of the 355 equity funds that started the race in 1970—only ⁸/₁₀ of

1 percent—have both survived and mounted a record of sustained excellence. Identified in Exhibit 8.2 as funds 4, 6, and 8, I now salute them by name: Davis New York Venture, Fidelity Contrafund, and Franklin Mutual Shares. Hail to the victors!

―――――――――――――― ⌒ ――――――――――――――

Only three out of the 355 equity funds that started the race in 1970—$\frac{8}{10}$ of 1 percent— have survived and mounted a record of sustained excellence.

―――――――――――――――――――――――――――――――

Significantly, while the portfolio managers for these three funds have changed over the years, the changes have been infrequent. Succeeding his father Shelby C. Davis, Chris Davis has managed the Davis Fund since 1991 (since 1996, with Kenneth Feinberg). Will Danoff has been the lead manager of Fidelity Contrafund since 1990, and Michael Price managed Franklin until 1997, followed by a successor who ran the fund until 2005.

But before you rush out to invest in these three funds with such truly remarkable long-term records, think about the *next* 35 years. Think about the odds that they will continue to outperform. Think about their present size. Think about the fact that within that time frame they are all virtually certain to have at least several new managers. Think, too, about the odds that these funds will even exist

35 years hence. It is a changing and competitive world out there in mutual fund land, and no one knows what the future holds. But I wish these managers and the shareholders of the funds they run the very best of luck.

~

Before you rush out to invest in these three funds with such truly remarkable long-term records, think about the next 35 years.

Conspicuous by its absence from this list of winning funds is Legg Mason Value Trust, managed since its 1982 inception by legendary investment professional supreme, Bill Miller. Since the fund did not begin operations until 1982, it is not on my list. But it provides several lessons about fund performance. Miller, something of a contrarian, is the only manager in the past four decades to outperform the S&P 500 for a truly remarkable 15 consecutive years (1991 to 2005, inclusive). Despite his great ability, the ever-humble Miller would be, I think, the first to agree with the late Harvard University paleontologist Stephen Jay Gould's tenet that "long streaks are extraordinary luck imposed on great skill."

Just like Joe DiMaggio's remarkable 56-game hitting streak in baseball, the longer Miller's streak extended, the more attention it got, and the more investor dollars flowed into the fund. But in 2006, his streak came to an end, even as did the streak of the Yankee Clipper years earlier. With the S&P 500 up 15.8 percent in 2006, Legg Mason Value was up only 5.8 percent, trailing the index by 10.0 percentage points, putting something of a dent in the long-term record.

Through 2005, the fund's annual rate of return had averaged 15.3 percent per year, compared with 12.9 percent for the S&P 500, a nice annual edge of 2.4 percentage points. But by 2006, the gap had shrunk to 1.9 percentage points, with an annual time-weighted return averaging 14.9 percent, compared with 13.0 percent for the index. Unsurprisingly, the major inflows of investor capital did not begin until 1997, the seventh year of the streak. So the actual return earned by Legg Mason Value's shareholders was a sharply lower 10.3 percent, far below its reported return. Is Miller's reversion toward and then below the market mean temporary or enduring? Will the fund be afflicted with the same malaise that attacked six of those nine long-term winners just discussed? Or is it merely a brief interval of bad luck. Who can know?

Whatever the case, the odds in favor of owning a consistently successful equity fund are less than one out of a hundred. However one slices and dices the data, there can be no question that funds with long-serving portfolio managers and records of consistent excellence are the exception rather than the rule in the mutual fund industry. The simple fact is that selecting a mutual fund that will outpace the stock market over the long term is, using Cervantes' wonderful observation, like "looking for a needle in the haystack." So I offer you Bogle's corollary: *"Don't look for the needle in the haystack. Just buy the haystack!"*

Funds with long-serving portfolio managers and records of consistent excellence are the exception rather than the rule in the mutual fund industry.

The haystack, of course, is the entire stock market portfolio, readily available through a low-cost index fund. The return of such a fund would have roughly matched or exceeded the returns of 346 of the 355 funds that began the 35-year competition described earlier in this chapter. And I see no reason that the same fund cannot achieve a roughly commensurate achievement in the years to come—not through any legerdemain, but merely through the relentless rules of arithmetic that you now must know so well.

We know that the index fund will deliver substantially all of the stock market's return. But with all the fund manager changes that will inevitably be forthcoming for actively managed funds; with all the funds that will die; with the successful funds drawing capital in amounts that will preclude their future success; and with our inability to be certain how much of a fund's performance is based on luck and how much on skill, there is simply no way to assure success by picking the funds that will beat the market, even by looking to their past performance over the long term. In fund performance, the past is rarely prologue.

Don't Take My Word for It

Need more advice? With his customary wisdom, **Paul Samuelson** sums up the difficulty of selecting superior managers in this parable. "Suppose it was demonstrated that one out of twenty alcoholics could learn to become a moderate social drinker. The experienced clinician would answer, 'Even if true, act as if it were false, for you will never identify that one in twenty, and in the attempt five in twenty will be ruined.' *Investors should forsake the search for such tiny needles in huge haystacks.*"

In the *Wall Street Journal*, long-time "Getting Going" columnist **Jonathan Clements** asks, "Can you pick the winners?" The answer: "Even fans of actively managed funds often concede that most other investors would be better off in index funds. But buoyed by abundant self-confidence, these folks aren't about to give up on actively managed funds themselves. A tad delusional? I think so. Picking the best-performing funds is 'like trying to predict the dice before you roll them down the craps

(continued)

table,' says an investment adviser in Boca Raton, FL. 'I can't do it. The public can't do it.'

"Still, I figure we shouldn't discourage fans of actively managed funds. With all their buying and selling, active investors ensure the market is reasonably efficient. That makes it possible for the rest of us to do the sensible thing, which is to index. Want to join me in this parasitic behavior? To build a well-diversified portfolio, you might stash 70 percent of your stock portfolio into a (Dow Jones) Wilshire 5000-index fund and the remaining 30 percent in an international-index fund."

If these comments don't persuade you about the hazards of focusing on past returns of mutual funds, just believe what fund organizations tell you. Every single firm in the fund industry acknowledges my conclusion that past fund performance is of no help in projecting the future returns of mutual funds. In every mutual fund prospectus, in every sales promotional folder, and in every mutual fund advertisement (albeit in print almost too small to read), the following warning appears: "Past performance is no guarantee of future results." Believe it!

Chapter Nine

Yesterday's Winners, Tomorrow's Losers

~

Fooled by Randomness*

IN SELECTING MUTUAL FUNDS, most fund investors seem to rely, not on sustained performance over the long term, but on exciting performance over the short term. (Exhibits 5.2 and 5.3 in Chapter 5 reinforce this point.) Studies show that 95 percent of all investor dollars flow to funds rated four or five stars by Morningstar, the statistical service most broadly used by investors in evaluating fund returns.

These "star ratings" are based on a composite of a fund's record over the previous 3-, 5-, and 10-year periods. (For younger funds, the ratings may cover as few as

---

* The title of a provocative book by Nassim Nicholas Taleb.

three years.) As a result, the previous two years' performance alone accounts for 35 percent of the rating of a fund with 10 years of history and 66 percent for a fund in business from three to five years, a heavy bias in favor of recent short-term returns.

How successful are fund choices based on the number of stars awarded for such short-term achievements? Not very! According to investment analyst Mark Hulbert, a mutual fund portfolio continuously adjusted to hold only Morningstar's five-star funds earned an annual return of just 6.9 percent between 1994 and 2004, nearly 40 percent below the 11.0 percent return on the Total Stock Market Index.* To make matters worse, according to Hulbert, these highly rated funds were assuming even more risk than the market (average monthly volatility in asset value: 16 percent for the funds compared with 15 percent for the stock market).

Sadly, the orientation of fund investors toward recent short-term returns works worst in strong bull markets. Exhibit 9.1 shows the top 10 performers among the 851 equity funds in operation during the great "new economy" market bubble of 1997 to 1999. A wondrous group

---

* In fairness, in 2002 Morningstar changed the basis for its rating system to reflect performance versus peers with similar objectives, rather than funds as a group. The relative performance of the four- and five-star funds has improved since then.

EXHIBIT 9.1   Picking the Short-Term Winners: Annual Returns, 1997–2002

	1997–1999		2000–2002	
Rank*		Time-Weighted	Rank*	Time-Weighted
1. Rydex OTC		65.8%	841.	−37.1%
2. RS Emerging Growth		62.5	832.	−31.2
3. MorganStanley Capital Op		59.5	845.	−40.7
4. Janus Olympus		58.5	791.	−27.4
5. Janus Twenty		54.8	801.	−28.6
6. Managers Capital Appreciation		53.3	798.	−28.2
7. Janus Mercury		51.5	790.	−27.2
8. Fidelity Aggressive Growth		51.5	843.	−39.1
9. Van Wagoner Emerging Growth		50.0	851.	−51.7
10. WM Growth		49.7	793.	−27.9
Average		55%		-34%

* Based on 851 funds with more than $100 million of assets.

they were! Focused on Internet, telecom, and technology stocks, these funds generated an average return of 55 per-cent *per year* during the upswing—a cumulative return of 279 percent for the full three years. Remarkable!

───────────── ∿ ─────────────

"The first shall be last." And they were.

─────────────────────────────

Well, you can guess what came next. The bubble burst, and, one by one, just as the Good Book warns, "The first shall be last." Over the next three years (2000 to 2002 inclu-sive), every one of the original top 10 funds plummeted into the bottom 60, with not a single fund in the original top 10 ranked higher than 790. Fund 9 on the upside actually was last—851 on the downside. Fund 1 dropped in rank to 841; fund 2 dropped to 832, and fund 3 tumbled to 845. On average, the one-time 10 top funds in the bull market were outperformed by 95 percent of their peers in the bear market that followed. For investors who believed that the past would be prologue, it was not a pretty result.

Please remember that even a single annual gain of 55 percent followed by a loss of 34 percent doesn't leave the investor with a 21 percent gain. More like 2 percent. (Do the arithmetic.) And with 3 years of average annual gains of 55 percent on the upside and annual losses averaging 34 percent on the downside (Exhibit 9.2), it was much worse. These aggressive new-economy funds ended up with a cumulative positive return averaging 13 percent for the full 6-year period, a far cry from the S&P 500's cumulative gain of 30 percent. Yet while that return was not particularly satisfactory in terms of the traditional returns reported by the average equity fund, it was hardly a disaster.

But for the shareholders of the funds, it was a disaster. By investing after seeing those mouth-watering cumulative returns that had averaged almost 280 percent, achieved in a soaring bull market, nearly all the buyers of these funds had missed the upside. Then, not a moment too soon, they caught the full force of the downside. Their funds tumbled by an astonishing average of 70 per-

EXHIBIT 9.2   Picking the Short-Term Winners: Cumulative Returns, 1997–2002

Rank*	Time-Weighted			Dollar-Weighted
	1996–1999	1999–2002	1996–2002	1996–2002
1. Rydex OTC	356%	–75%	13%	–62%
2. RS Emerging Growth	329	–67	39	–80
3. Morgan Stanley Capital Op	305	–79	–16	–85
4. Janus Olympus	298	–62	52	–57
5. Janus Twenty	271	–64	35	–18
6. Managers Capital Appreciation	260	–63	33	–60
7. Janus Mercury	248	–61	34	–56
8. Fidelity Aggressive Growth	247	–77	–21	–87
9. Van Wagoner Emerging Growth	237	–89	–62	–66
10. WM Growth	235	–62	26	–3
Average	279%	–70%	13%	–57%

*Based on 851 funds with more than $100 million of assets.

cent during the next three years. Result: While the funds themselves achieved a net *gain* of 13 percent, the investors in these funds incurred a *loss* of 57 percent. By investing in these once high-flying funds, more than half of the capital that investors had placed in these hot funds had gone up in smoke. The message is clear: *avoid performance chasing based on short-term returns, especially during great bull markets.*

Though the results are hardly as dramatic, the "don't chase past performance" principle also holds during more sedate stock markets. In my first book, *Bogle on Mutual Funds*, I compared the records of the 20 top-performing mutual funds during each year from 1982 through 1992 with their records in the subsequent year (Exhibit 9.3). As it happened, the top 20 funds of that ranked number one in each year had a subsequent average ranking of 284 among the list

EXHIBIT 9.3 Reversion to the Mean: Top 20 Funds, 1982–1992 and 1995–2005

	1982–1992		1995–2005	
Rank	Average Follow-Up Rank	Performance Percentile*	Average Follow-Up Rank	Performance Percentile*
1.	100	85%	949	34%
2.	383	44	875	39
3.	231	66	720	50
4.	343	50	649	55
5.	358	47	626	56
6.	239	65	787	45
7.	220	68	702	51
8.	417	39	604	58
9.	242	64	308	79
10.	330	52	593	59
11.	310	54	581	60
12.	262	62	731	49
13.	271	60	585	59
14.	207	70	426	70
15.	271	60	712	51
16.	287	58	387	73
17.	332	51	493	66
18.	348	49	541	62
19.	310	54	522	64
20.	226	67	591	59
Average	284	58%	619	57%

*Percentile 100 is best.

of 681 funds, outpacing 58 percent of their peers, or barely above average. During that period, the highest achievement on the 20-fund list was turned in by the number one funds, which averaged a rank of 100 in the subsequent year.

The clear reversion to the mean suggested by that single test represented powerful evidence that winning performance by a mutual fund is unlikely to be repeated. But there was no reason (except common sense) to assume that the 1982 to 1992 experience would recur. So, just for fun, I repeated the test in 2006, beginning with the top-performing 20 funds in 1995 and the top 20 funds in each of the nine subsequent years. I then checked the rank of each fund in the following year, just as before.

In general, the results were remarkably similar. The average subsequent rank of the top 20 funds from 1995 through 2005 was 619, outpacing 57 percent of their peers and barely above the average fund among the 1,440 fund total—just as in the prior test. In an interesting reversal of fortune, however, the number one funds of that era turned out to have, not the highest subsequent ranking, but the lowest ranking among the top 20. These champions subsequently earned an average ranking of 949 among the 1,440-fund total, outpacing only 34 percent of their peers. While "the first can be first" sometimes, the first can be last at other times, a wonderful illustration of the inevitable randomness of fund performance.

———————————— ❦ ————————————

The stars produced in the mutual fund field are rarely stars; all too often they are comets.

———————————————————————————

The message is clear: reversion to the mean (RTM)—in this case, the tendency of funds whose records substantially exceed industry norms to return to average or below—is alive and well in the mutual fund industry. In stock market blow-offs, "the first shall be last." But in more typical environments, reversion to the fund mean—which, as we have seen in earlier chapters, substantially lags the return earned by a stock market index fund—is the rule. So please remember that the stars produced in the mutual fund field are rarely stars; all too often they are comets, lighting up the firmament for a brief moment in time and then flaming out, their ashes floating gently to earth.

With each passing year, the reality is increasingly clear. Fund returns seem to be random. Yes, there are rare cases where skill seems to be involved, but it would require decades to determine how much of a fund's success can be attributed to luck, and how much attributed to skill. And by then, you might ask yourself questions like these: (1) How long will that manager, with that staff and with that strategy, remain on the job? (2) If the fund's assets are many times larger at the end of the period than at the beginning, will the same results that were attractive in the first place be sustained? (3) Will the stock market continue to favor the same kinds of stocks that have been at the heart of the manager's style? In short, selecting mutual funds on the basis of short-term performance is all too likely to be hazardous duty, and it is almost always destined to produce returns that fall far short of those achieved by the stock market, itself so easily achievable through an index fund.

Don't Take My Word for It

Listen to **Nassim Nicholas Taleb,** author of *Fooled by Randomness:* "Toss a coin; *heads* and the manager will make $10,000 over the year, *tails* and he will lose $10,000. We run [the contest] for the first year [for 10,000 managers]. At the end of the year, we expect 5,000 managers to be up $10,000 each, and 5,000 to be down $10,000. Now we run the game a second year. Again, we can expect 2,500 managers to be up two years in a row; another year, 1,250; a fourth one, 625; a fifth, 313. We have now, simply in a fair game, 313 managers who made money for five years in a row. [And in 10 years, just 10 of the original 10,000 managers.] Out of pure luck.... A population entirely composed of bad managers will produce a small amount of great track

(continued)

records. . . . The number of managers with great track records in a given market depends far more on the number of people who started in the investment business (in place of going to dental school), rather than on their ability to produce profits."

That may sound theoretical, so here is a practical outlook. Hear *Money* magazine's colloquy with **Ted Aronson,** partner of respected Philadelphia money management firm Aronson+Johnson+Ortiz:

Q. You've said that investing in an actively managed fund (as opposed to a passively run index fund) is an act of faith. What do you mean?

A. Under normal circumstances, it takes between 20 and 800 years [of monitoring performance] to statistically prove that a money manager is skillful, not lucky. To be 95 percent certain that a manager is not just lucky, it can easily take nearly a millennium—which is a lot more than most people have in mind when they say "long-term." Even to be only 75 percent sure he's skillful, you'd generally have to track a manager's performance for between 16 and 115 years. . . . Investors need to know how the money management business really works. It's a stacked deck. The game is unfair.

Q. Where do you invest?

A. In Vanguard index funds. I've owned Vanguard Index 500 for 23 years. Once you throw in taxes, it just skewers the argument for active management. Personally, I think indexing wins hands-down. After tax, active management just can't win."

Finally, *Money* magazine columnist and author **Jason Zweig** sums up performance chasing in a single pungent sentence: "Buying funds based purely on their past performance is one of the stupidest things an investor can do."

Chapter Ten

Seeking Advice to Select Funds?

Look before You Leap.

THE EVIDENCE PRESENTED in Chapters 8 and 9 teaches two lessons: (1) Selecting winning equity funds over the long term bears all the potential success of looking for the needle in the haystack; and (2) Selecting winning funds based on their performance over relatively short-term periods in the past is all too likely to lead, if not to disaster, at least to disappointment.

So why not abandon these "do-it-yourself" approaches, and rely on professional advice? Pick a financial consultant (the designation usually given to the stockbrokers of Wall Street, and indeed brokers everywhere) or an investment adviser (the designation usually applied to nonbrokers, who often—but not always—work on a "fee only," rather than a commission, basis).

I'll attempt to answer that question in this chapter. But first, I want to note that I'm focusing only on the ability of advisers to help you select equity funds that can produce superior returns for your portfolio. Professional investment advisers provide many other services including asset allocation, information on tax considerations, and advice on how to save while you work and on how to spend when you retire; and they are always there to consult with you about the financial markets.

Advisers can encourage you to prepare for the future and can help you deal with many extra-investment decisions that have investment implications (for example, when you want to build a fund for your children's college education or need to raise cash for the purchase of a home). Experienced advisers can also help you avoid the potholes along the investment highway. (Put more grossly, they may help you avoid making such dumb mistakes as chasing past performance or trying to time the market.) At their best, these important services can enhance the implementation of your investment program.

The overwhelming majority of investors rely on brokers or advisers for help in penetrating the dense fog of complexity that, for better or worse, permeates our financial system. If the generally accepted estimate that some 70 percent of the 55 million American families who invest in mutual funds do so through intermediaries is correct, then only about 15 million families choose the "do-it-yourself" road. The remaining 40 million families rely on professional helpers. (That's the unsuccessful strategy described in my opening parable about the Gotrocks family.)

We'll never know exactly how much value is added—or subtracted—by these helpers. But it's hard for me to imagine that as a group they are other than, well, average. That is, their advice on equity fund selection produces returns for their clients that are probably not measurably different from those of the average fund, some 2.5 percentage points per year behind the stock market, as measured by the S&P 500 Index (see Chapter 4).

I'm willing to consider the possibility that the fund selections recommended by advisers may be better than average. As I'll explain in Chapter 11, if they merely select funds with the lowest all-in costs—hardly rocket science—they'll do better for you. If they're savvy enough to realize that high-turnover funds are highly tax-inefficient, they'll pick up important additional savings for you in transaction costs and taxes. If they put those two strategies together and emphasize low-cost index funds—as so many advisers do—so much the better for their clients.

And if professional investment consultants are wise enough—or lucky enough—to keep their clients from jumping on the latest and hottest bandwagon (for example, the new economy craze of the late 1990s, reflected in the mania for funds investing in technology, telecommunications, and Internet stocks), their clients could earn returns that easily surpass the disappointing returns achieved by fund investors as a group. Remember the additional shortfall of 2.7 percentage points per year relative to the average equity fund that was estimated in Chapter 5? To remind you, the nominal return of fund investors came to just 7.3 percent per year during 1980 to 2005, despite a wonderful stock market in which a simple S&P 500 Index Fund earned a return of 12.3 percent.

Alas (from the standpoint of the advisers), there is simply no evidence that the fund selection advice they provide has produced any better returns than those achieved by fund investors on average. In fact, the evidence goes the other way. A recent study by a research team led by two Harvard Business School professors concluded that, during between 1996 and 2002 alone, "the underperformance of broker-channel funds (adviser-sold) relative to funds sold through the direct channel (purchased directly by investors) cost investors approximately $9 billion per year."

———————————— ∼ ————————————

**Average return of funds recommended
by advisors: 2.9 percent per year.
For equity funds purchased directly: 6.6 percent.**

————————————————————————————————

Specifically, the study found that adviser asset allocations were no better, that they chased market trends, and that those they advised paid higher upfront charges. The study's conclusion: *the weighted average return of equity funds held by investors who relied on advisers (excluding all charges paid up front or at the time of redemption)— averaged just 2.9 percent per year—compared with 6.6 percent earned by investors who took charge of their own affairs.*

This powerful evidence, however, does not bring the researchers to the clear conclusion that advice in its totality has negative value: "We remain," the report states, "open to the possibility that substantial intangible benefits exist, and will undertake more research to identify these intangible benefits and explore the elite group of advisers who do improve the welfare of households who trust them."

There is other powerful evidence that the use of stockbrokers (as distinct from financial advisers) has a strong negative impact on the returns earned by fund investors. In a study prepared for Fidelity Investments covering the 10-year period 1994 to 2003 inclusive, broker-managed funds had the lowest ratings relative to their peers of any group of funds. (The other groups included funds operated by privately owned managers, by publicly-owned managers, by managers owned by financial conglomerates, and by bank managers.)

The Merrill Lynch funds were 18 percentage points below the fund industry average; the Goldman Sachs and Morgan Stanley funds were 9 percentage points below average; and both the Wells Fargo and Smith Barney funds were 8 percentage points behind. Part of the reason for this disturbing performance may arise from the nature of the job. The brokerage firm and its brokers/financial consultants must sell something every single day. When the firm introduces a new fund, the brokers have to sell it to someone. (Imagine a day when nobody sold anything, and the stock market lay fallow, silent all day long.)

A Merrill Lynch example illustrates the destructive challenges that are often faced by investors who rely on stockbrokers. In March 2000, just as the bubble created by the Internet stock craze reached at its peak, Merrill Lynch, the world's largest stock brokerage firm, jumped on the bandwagon with two new funds to sell. Both were "new economy" funds. One was a "Focus Twenty" fund (based on the then-popular theory that if a manager's 100 favorite stocks were good, surely his 20 favorites would be even better). The other was an "Internet Strategies" fund. The public offering of the two funds was an incredible success. Merrill's brokers pulled in $2.0 billion from their trusting (or was it performance chasing?) clients, $0.9 billion in Focus Twenty and $1.1 billion in Internet Strategies.

The subsequent returns of the funds, however, were an incredible failure. (Not surprising: the best time to sell a new fund to investors—when it's hot—is often the worst time to buy it.) Internet Strategies tanked almost immediately. Its asset value dropped 61 percent during the remainder of 2000 and another 62 percent by October 2001. The total loss was a cool 86 percent as most of its investors cashed out their shares at staggering losses. When the fund's original $1.1 billion of assets had plummeted to just $128 million, Merrill decided to kill Internet Strategies and give it a decent burial, merging it with another Merrill fund. (Keeping a record like that alive would have been a continuing embarrassment to the firm.)

$\sim$

Two new Merrill Lynch funds: a marketing success for the firm; an utter failure for its clients.

For what it is worth, the losses in Focus Twenty were less severe. Its asset value declined 28 percent in the remainder of 2000, another 70 percent in 2001, and another 39 percent in 2002, before finally posting positive returns in the three years that followed. On balance, its cumulative lifetime return through late 2006 came to minus 79 percent. Investors have regularly withdrawn their capital, and the fund's assets, which would reach almost $1.5 billion in 2000, currently languish at $82 million, a 95 percent decline. But, unlike its Internet Strategies cousin, Focus Twenty soldiers on. The lesson remains: The $2 billion marketing success of the Merrill Lynch Internet Strategies fund and Focus Twenty fund was an utter failure for their clients, who lost some 80 percent of their hard-earned savings.

The *New York Times* contest: Funds chosen by advisers earned 40 percent less than an index fund.

A more extensive test of the ability of financial advisers to outpace the S&P 500 Index was initiated by the *New York Times* in July 1993. The editors asked five respected advisers (none were brokers) how they would invest $50,000 in a tax-free retirement account holding mutual fund shares for an investor who had a time horizon of at least 20 years. The comparative standard would be the returns earned by Vanguard 500 Index Fund.

Each quarter, the *Times* faithfully published the records of the index fund and the advisers, tracking their initial portfolios and the subsequent changes they made. By 2000, seven years later, the *Times* reported their accomplishments (Exhibit 10.1). The hypothetical $50,000

EXHIBIT 10.1   Fund Advisers versus the Vanguard 500 Index, July 1993–June 2000

Investment Method	Final Profit
Eric Kobren, Fidelity Insight	$105,093
Sheldon Jacobs, No-Load Fund Investor	102,209
Jack A. Brill, "Socially Responsible" Investor	100,082
Russel Kinnel, Morningstar	73,487
Harold R. Evensky, Investment Adviser	61,816
Average	$188,500
Index 500	$138,750

Note: Total value of an initial $50,000 investment.

portfolios run by the advisers had turned in a profit, on average, of $188,500 on June 30, 2000. (The highest profit was $105,100; the lowest, $61,800.)

While the editors properly acknowledged that not one of these advisers was able to outpace the result of the Vanguard 500 Index Fund, they failed to report its final profit based on that initial investment of $50,000. The answer (which I provided to the paper in a subsequent letter to the editor) was $138,750. That is, the average adviser produced a paper profit on his portfolio of recommended funds that was about 40 percent less than the profit on the index fund.

In mid-2000, the *Times* abruptly terminated the contest without notice. I do not know why, since the original stated intention was to make a 20-year evaluation.* But I can guess either that the advisers were too embarrassed to continue to participate in the contest, or that, as the differential in favor of the passively managed index fund grew, quarter after quarter, the contest became sort of non-newsworthy—even boring. I also have no idea why the *New York Times* determined that the remarkable differential in favor of the index fund was *not* "news that's fit to print."

I endorse the idea that for many—indeed, most—investors, financial advisers may provide a valuable service in giving you peace of mind, in helping you establish a sensible fund portfolio that matches your appetite for reward and your tolerance for risk, and in helping you stay the course in troubled waters. But the evidence I've presented so far strongly confirms my original hypothesis

---

* We'll never know what would have happened had the contest continued. But the fact is that the *Times* terminated it at the very peak of the bull market, and at the moment of triumph for the index fund. Since then, the index fund, like the market itself, has barely held its own. While we don't know whether the advisers would have changed their portfolios, we can calculate how those funds they held in 2000 have since performed. Two advisers did considerably better than the index fund during that subsequent period; one was worse, and one about the same. (The results of the fifth adviser can't be measured, because two of the funds in his portfolio went out of business.) Despite this all-too-typical reversion to the mean, the index fund maintained its superiority for the full period, with a final profit of $131,800 compared with $117,700 for the fund portfolio of the average adviser, surpassing the results of three of the four remaining advisers.

that, vital as those services may be, advisers as a group cannot be credibly relied on to add value by selecting winning funds for you.

Here is a final piece of compelling evidence to support that thesis. Mark Hulbert, editor of the *Hulbert Financial Digest,* has been monitoring the real-time records of financial advisers who report their recommendations in newsletters subscribed to by investors. He has tracked the performance of these advisers over the past 26 years, and here's what he finds:

- Of the 35 newsletters that existed in 1980, only 13 are still in business today. Only three outperformed the market over the subsequent 26 years.
- Of the other 22 advisers, only two were ahead of the S&P 500 Index when they discontinued publication.
- An initial $100,000 investment in the S&P 500 Index 26 years ago would be worth nearly $2,500,000 today. By way of contrast, a similar investment in the portfolios managed by the advisers tracked by Hulbert would be worth about $1,400,000.

Hulbert's conclusion: "You can outperform more than 80 percent of your fellow investors over the next several decades simply by investing in an index fund—and doing nothing else."

--- ∽ ---

Index funds endure, while most advisers and funds do not.

These examples surely reinforce the thesis that index funds endure, while most advisers and funds do not; that index fund returns strongly exceed the returns earned even by those advisers and funds that do survive; that the odds against successful fund selection by advisers are large, and that compounding these rather consistent differentials in rates of annual return mount up to truly staggering differences in wealth accumulation over the long term.

If you consider the selection of an adviser, please take heed of these findings. If you decide to go ahead, make sure you are paying a fair fee (which results in a deduction from whatever rate of return your fund portfolio earns). Since most investment advisory fees tend to begin in the range of 1 percent per year, be sure to balance the worth of the peripheral services that advisers provide against the reduction in your returns that those fees are likely to represent over time. Finally—and this will hardly surprise you—look with particular favor on advisers who recommend stock and bond index funds in their model portfolios.

Don't Take My Word for It

Listen, once again, to the widely respected invest-ment adviser **William Bernstein,** who writes in *The Four Pillars of Investment Wisdom* as follows: "You will want to ensure that your adviser is choosing your investments purely on their investment merit and not on the basis of how the vehicles reward him. The warning signs here are recommendations of load funds, insurance products, limited partner-ships, or separate accounts. The best, and only, way to make sure that you and your adviser are on the same team is to make sure that he is 'fee-only,' that is, that he receives no remuneration from any other source besides you. . . . 'Fee-only' is not without pit-falls, however. Your adviser's fees should be reason-able. It is simply not worth paying anybody more than 1 percent to manage your money. Above $1 million, you should be paying no more than 0.75 percent, and above $5 million, no more than 0.5 percent. . . . Your adviser should use index/passive stock funds wherever possible. If he tells you that he is able to find managers who can beat the indexes, he is fooling both you and himself. I refer to a com-mitment to passive indexing as 'asset-class religion.' Don't hire anyone without it."

Chapter Eleven

Focus on the Lowest-Cost Funds

~

*The More the Managers Take,
the Less the Investors Make.*

WHAT LESSONS HAVE YOU learned in Chapters 8 through 10? Selecting equity funds based on long-term past performance hasn't been the answer. Selecting funds based on past short-term performance hasn't been the answer either. Relying on even the best-intentioned financial advice seems to work only spasmodically. How can successful fund selection prove so difficult? Because of something that, deep down, our common sense tells us: *Performance comes and goes.*

But there is also something else worth knowing: you can be more successful in selecting winning funds by focusing, not on the inevitable evanescence of past performance, but on something that seems to go on forever or, more fairly, a factor that has persisted over all the fund industry's long history. That factor is the *costs* of owning mutual funds. *Costs go on forever.*

Common sense tells us that performance comes and goes, but costs go on forever.

One major cost is the fund's expense ratio, and it tends to change little over time. While some funds scale down their fee rates as assets grow, the reductions are usually sufficiently modest that high-cost funds tend to remain high-cost; lower-cost funds tend to remain lower-cost, and the few very low-cost funds tend to remain very low-cost. The average-cost funds, too, tend to persist in that category.

Another large cost of equity fund ownership is the sales charge paid on each purchase of shares. It, too, tends to persist. Load funds rarely become no-load funds, and vice versa. (I can recall no large fund organization making the immediate conversion from a load to a no-load distribution system since Vanguard took that drastic and unprecedented step 30 years ago.)

The portfolio turnover costs of individual funds also tend to persist. Transactions cost money, and we estimate that turnover costs are roughly 0.5 percent on each purchase and sale, meaning that a fund with 100 percent portfolio turnover would carry a cost to shareholders of about 1 percent of assets, year after year. Similarly, 50 percent turnover would cost about 0.50 percent; and 10 percent turnover would cost about 0.10 percent, and so on. Rule of thumb: turnover costs equal 1 percent of the turnover rate.

Most comparisons of fund costs rely solely on reported expense ratios, and uniformly find that higher costs are associated with lower returns. This pattern holds not only for equity funds as a group, but in each of the nine Morningstar style boxes (large-, mid-, and small-cap funds, each sorted into fund groups with growth, value, and blended objectives). While few independent comparisons take into account the additional cost of fund portfolio turnover, a similar relationship exists. Funds in the low-turnover quartile have consistently outperformed those in the high-turnover quartile for all equity funds as a group, and in each of the nine style boxes.

Adding that estimated turnover cost to each fund's expense ratio makes the relationship sheer dynamite. Taking into account both costs, we find that the all-in annual costs range from 0.9 percent of assets in the lowest-cost quartile to 3.0 percent in the highest-cost quartile as shown in Exhibit 11.1. (This exercise ignores sales charges and, therefore overstates the net returns earned by the funds in each quartile.)

Costs matter! That 2.1 percentage point difference constitutes a huge portion of the 2.7 point advantage in the returns among the lowest-cost funds over the highest-cost funds during the past 10 years. Net annual return of low-cost funds, 11.7 percent; net annual return of high-cost funds, just 9.0 percent, a 30 percent enhancement in each year's return achieved simply by relying on relative costs as a guide to performance success.

Also note that in each of the fund quartiles, when we add the costs to the funds' reported net returns, the gross annual returns earned in each category are virtually identical. Pre-cost returns fall into a narrow range: a high of 12.8 percent for the third quartile and a low of 12.0 percent for the fourth quartile, just what we might expect. Costs account for most of the difference in the annual net returns earned by the funds.

And there is another significant difference. Step by step, as costs increase, so does risk (using the volatility of monthly returns relative to the volatility of the S&P 500 Index as the measure). Those highest-expense, highest-turnover-cost funds assumed fully 34 percent more risk than their lowest-cost cousins. If you take that reduction in risk into account, the risk-adjusted annual return for

EXHIBIT 11.1 Equity Mutual Funds: Returns versus Costs, 1995–2005

Cost Quartile	Gross Return	Costs	Net Return	Risk	Risk-Adjusted Return	Cumulative Gain
One (lowest)	12.6%	0.9%	11.7%	16.0%	11.9%	207%
Two	12.5	1.5	11.0	17.0	10.9	181
Three	12.8	2.0	10.8	18.5	10.1	163
Four (highest)	12.0	3.0	9.0	21.4	8.1	118
Average fund	12.5%	1.9%	10.6%	18.2%	9.8%	154%
Low cost enhancement	+5%	−70%	+30%	−34%	+47%	+75%
500 Index Fund	11.4%	0.2%	11.2%	15.7%	11.4%	194%

Note: Costs include expense ratios and estimated turnover costs but exclude sales loads. Gross return was calculated by adding these costs back into each group's net return.

the low-cost quartile comes to 11.9 percent, fully 47 percent higher than the 8.1 percent risk-adjusted return of the high-cost quartile.

When we compound those annual returns over time, the cumulative difference reaches staggering proportions. Total compound gain for the period: 207 percent for the low-cost funds, 118 percent for the high-cost funds, a near doubling of profit arising almost entirely from the cost differential. Talk about the relentless rules of humble arithmetic!

In other words, the final value of the low-cost funds more than tripled over the decade, whereas the value of the high-cost funds barely doubled. Surely "fishing in the low-cost pond" should enhance your returns, and by a wide margin at that. Again, yes, costs matter!

But if you are seeking the lowest-cost funds, why limit the search to actively managed funds? The classic index fund had the lowest costs of all: an expense ratio averaging 0.2 percent per year during this period. With no measurable turnover costs, its total all-in costs were but 0.2 percent. The gross return of the 500 Index Fund was 11.4 percent per year; the net return 11.2 percent. Carrying a lower risk than any of the four cost quartiles (annual price volatility averaging 15.7 percent), its risk-adjusted annual return was 11.4 percent, for a cumulative risk-adjusted gain that was about in the middle of the top quartile.

─────────── ～ ───────────

The index fund's risk-adjusted return: 194 percent; average managed fund, 154 percent.

───────────────────────────────

The index fund's compound risk-adjusted profit of 194 percent surpassed the 154 percent compound profit earned by the average fund by about one-third, all the more impressive since that average is overstated (as always) by the fact that only the funds that were good enough to survive the decade are included in the data. What's more, selecting the index fund eliminated the need to look for those rare needles in the market haystack represented by the very few active funds that have performed better than that haystack, in the often-vain hope that their winning ways will continue over decades yet to come.

If investors could rely on only a single factor to select future superior performers and to avoid future inferior performers, it would be fund costs. The record could hardly be clearer: *the more the managers and brokers take, the less the investors make.* So why not own an index fund with no active manager and no management fee, and with virtually no trading of stocks through those Helpers mentioned in Chapter 1? Why not, indeed? Chapter 12 explores this idea further.

Don't Take My Word for It

Beginning as far back as 1995, **Tyler Mathisen,** then executive editor of *Money,* conceded the point: "For nearly two decades, John Bogle, the tart-tongued chairman of the Vanguard Group, has preached the virtues of index funds—those boring portfolios that aim to match the performance of a market barometer. And for much of that time, millions of fund investors (not to mention dozens of financial journalists including this one) basically ignored him. Sure, we recognized the intrinsic merits of index funds such as low annual expenses and because the funds keep turnover to a minimum, tiny transaction costs. Moreover, because index fund managers convert paper profits into realized gains less frequently than do the skippers of actively managed funds, shareholders pay less tax each year to Uncle Sam. To be sure, those three advantages form a trio as impressive as Domingo, Pavarotti, and Carreras.

"Well, Jack, we were wrong. You win. Settling for average is good enough, at least for a substantial portion of most investors' stock and bond portfolios. In fact, more often than not, aiming for benchmark-matching returns through index funds assures shareholders of a better-than-average chance of outperforming the typical managed stock or bond portfolio. It's the paradox of fund investing today:

Gunning for average is your best shot at finishing above average. We've come around to agreeing with the sometimes prickly, always provocative, fund exec known to admirers and detractors alike as Saint Jack: Indexing should form the core of most investors' fund portfolios. So here's to you, Jack. You have a right to call it, as you recently did in a booklet you wrote, *The Triumph of Indexing.*" (Thanks, Tyler!)

Chapter Twelve

Profit from the Majesty of Simplicity

Hold Index Funds That Own the Entire Stock Market.

— ◈ —

IF LOW COSTS ARE GOOD (and I don't think a single analyst, academic, or industry expert would disagree that low costs are good), why wouldn't it be logical to focus on the lowest-cost funds of all—index funds that own the entire stock market? Several index funds carry expense ratios as low as 0.10 percent or even less, and incur turnover costs that turn out to be zero. They have all-in costs of just 10 basis points per year, 80 percent lower even than the 90 basis points for the low-cost quartile of funds described in Chapter 11.

And it works. Witness the real-world superiority of the S&P 500 Index Fund compared with the average equity fund over the past 25 years and over the previous decade, as described in earlier chapters. The case for the success of indexing in the past is compelling and unarguable. And with the outlook for subdued returns on stocks during the decade ahead, I am concluding my anecdotal stroll through the relentless rules of humble arithmetic with a final statistical example that suggests what the future may hold.

We can, in fact, use statistics designed to project the odds that a passively managed index fund will outpace an actively managed equity fund over various time periods. The complex exercise is called the "Monte Carlo simulation."* What it does is make a few simple assumptions about the volatility of equity fund returns and the extent to which they vary from the returns earned in the stock market, as well as an assumption about the all-in costs of equity investing. The particular example presented here assumes that index fund costs will run to 0.25 percent per year and that the costs of active management will run to 2

---

*Basically, a Monte Carlo simulation takes all the monthly returns earned by stocks over a long period—even a full century—scrambles them randomly, and then computes the annual rates of return generated by each of the thousands of hypothetical portfolios.

percent per year. (Index funds are available at far lower costs, and the typical equity fund has even higher costs, so we've given actively managed funds the benefit of a very large doubt.)

Result: Over one year, about 29 percent of active managers on average, would be expected to outpace the index; over five years about 15 percent would be expected to win; over 10 years, 9 percent; over 25 years, 5 percent; and over 50 years just 2 percent of active managers would be expected to win (Exhibit 12.1).

How will the future actually play out? Of course, we can't be sure. But we know what the past 25 years look like, and we know that over the past 35 years only

EXHIBIT 12.1   Odds of Actively Managed Portfolio Outperforming Passive Index Fund

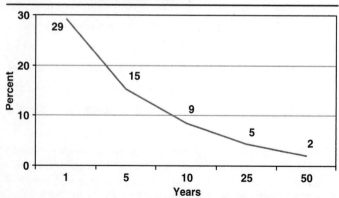

9 of the 355 funds in business at the outset outperformed the stock market index by more than 2 percent per year. What's more, even the majority of these winners lost their early edge a decade or more ago. So it looks as if our statistical odds are in the right ballpark. This arithmetic suggests—even demands—that index funds deserve an important place in your portfolio, even as they constitute the overriding portion of my own.

Whatever the case, in the era of subdued stock and bond market returns that most likely lies in prospect, fund costs will become more important than ever. Even more so when we move from the illusion that mutual funds as a group can capture whatever returns our financial markets provide to the even greater illusion that most mutual fund investors can capture even those depleted returns in their own fund portfolios. What the index fund has going for it is, as I have often said, "the magic of simplicity in an empire of parsimony."

To reiterate: all those pesky costs—fund expense ratios, sales charges, and turnover costs; tax costs; and the most subtle cost of all, the rising cost of living (inflation)—are virtually guaranteed to erode the spending power of our investments over time. What's more, only in the rarest cases do fund investors actually succeed in capturing the returns that the funds report.

~

**My conclusions rely on mathematical facts—
the relentless rules of humble arithmetic.**

My conclusions about the market returns we can expect in the years ahead, as well as my conclusions about the share of those returns that funds will capture, and the share of those returns that we investors will actually enjoy, have one thing in common: They rely, not on opinion, but largely on mathematical facts—the relentless rules of humble arithmetic that make selecting winning funds rather like looking for a needle in a haystack. You ignore these rules at your peril.

If the road to investment success is filled with dangerous turns and giant potholes, never forget that simple arithmetic can enable you to moderate those turns and avoid those potholes. So do your best to diversify to the nth degree; minimize your investment expenses; and focus your emotions where they cannot wreak the kind of havoc that most other people experience in their investment programs. Rely on your own common sense. Emphasize all-stock-market index funds. Carefully consider your risk tolerance and the portion of your investments you allocate to equities. Then stay the course.

───────────────── ∿ ─────────────────

**All index funds are not created equal.
One example: the difference
between $122,700 and $99,100.**

I should add, importantly, that all index funds are not created equal. While their index-based portfolios are substantially identical, their costs are anything but identical. Some have miniscule expense ratios; others have expense ratios that surpass the bounds of reason. Some are no-load funds, but nearly a third, as it turns out, have substantial front-end loads, often with an option to pay those loads over a period of (usually) five years; others entail the payment of a standard brokerage commission.

The gap between the costs charged by the low-cost funds and the high-cost funds offered by 10 major fund organizations for their S&P 500-Index-based funds runs upward of an amazing 1.2 percentage points per year. (Exhibit 12.2)

Today, there are some 115 index mutual funds designed to track the S&P 500 Index. Astonishingly, more than half of them carry an initial sales load, albeit often concealed by offering class "B" shares with no front-end load but with an additional heavy annual fee (used to pay the broker). The wise investor will select only those index funds that are available without sales loads, and those operating with the lowest costs. These costs—no surprise here!—are directly related to the net returns delivered to the shareholders of these funds.

EXHIBIT 12.2 Costs of Selected S&P 500 Index Funds

Five Low-Cost Index 500 Funds	Annual Expense Ratio	Annual Expense Ratio Including Any Sales Charges
1. Fidelity Spartan[a]	0.07%	0.07%
2. Vanguard Admiral[a]	0.09	0.09
3. Vanguard (Regular)	0.18	0.18
4. USAA	0.19	0.19
5. T. Rowe Price	0.35	0.35
Five High-Cost Funds[b]		
1. UBS	0.69%	1.45%
2. Morgan Stanley	0.64	1.40
3. Wells Fargo	0.64	1.39
4. Evergreen	0.56	1.31
5. J.P. Morgan	0.53	1.30

[a] Share classes available subject to initial minimum investments and/or specified holding periods.
[b] Investors pay the lower expense ratio only if they first pay an initial sales charge of about 5 percent.

In the past, some S&P 500-Index-based funds may have earned small increases in return (or been penalized by small reductions) based on their managers' ability (or inability) to employ strategies that allow small short-term departures from the exact weightings of the stocks in the index. I assume, however, that these variations will be lower in the future, and have therefore ignored them as an element in the cost-value equation. Funds tracking a particular index are—or should be—commodities in terms of their portfolios and the returns they provide. So variations in costs make the difference. While cost differentials may look trivial when expressed on an annual basis, compounded over the years they make the difference between investment success and failure.

In January 1984, the second index mutual fund was formed—Wells Fargo Equity Index Fund. Its subsequent return can be compared with that of the original Vanguard 500 Index Fund over the same period. Both funds selected the S&P 500 Index as their benchmark. The sales commission on the Vanguard Index 500 Fund was eliminated within months of its initial offering, and it has operated with an expense ratio averaging 0.28 percent annually. (By 2005, the ratio had decreased to 0.18 percent, and to 0.09 percent for longer-term investors and those who had $100,000 or more invested in the fund.) In contrast, the Wells Fargo fund carried an initial sales charge of 5.5 percent througout the period, and its expense ratio averaged 0.80 percent per year (0.64 percent in 2005).

These seemingly small differences added up to a 23 percent enhancement in value for the Vanguard fund. An original investment of $10,000 in each produced a profit of $122,700 for the Vanguard 500 Index Fund, compared with $99,100 for the Wells Fargo Equity Index Fund. *All index funds are not created equal.* Intelligent investors will select the lowest cost index funds that are available from reputable fund organizations.

---------------------- ∼ ----------------------

Your index fund should not be your manager's cash cow. It should be your own cash cow.

Some years ago, a Wells Fargo representative was asked how the firm could justify such high charges. The answer: "You don't understand. It's our cash cow." (That is, it regularly generates lots of profits for the manager.) By carefully selecting the lowest cost index funds for your portfolio, you can be sure that the fund is not the manager's cash cow, but your own.

Given my preference for the all-market index fund, I almost hesitate to tell you that, since that lonely first S&P Index was formed in 1975, a staggering total of another 578 more index funds of all sizes and shapes are now in operation. Investors face a mind-boggling set of confusing choices—large cap, mid-cap, small-cap, industry sectors, international, single country, and so on. To make it more confusing, indexing works like a charm in every one of these areas. A well-administered index fund is inevitably destined to surpass the returns earned by the other investors in the market segment tracked by its index. Even though we never have complete information about the precise returns earned by investors as a group in each segment, given the relentless rules of humble arithmetic, it *must* work that way.

Standard & Poor's Corporation now compares index returns with actual returns achieved by active managers in many U.S. market segments, and the results are unmistakable. Over the past five years alone, the S&P 500 Index has outpaced 67 percent of large-cap general equity funds, while the S&P Mid-Cap 400 Index has outperformed 84 percent of mid-cap funds, and the S&P Small-Cap 600 Index has outperformed 79 percent of all small-cap funds. Remarkable but unsurprising. While these comparisons, sorted by number of funds rather than by fund assets, have the flaws noted earlier, the message could hardly be clearer: indexing is the winning strategy.

Interestingly, Standard & Poor's tries to take survivor bias into account in its calculations. During the past five years alone, an astonishing 28 percent of all general equity funds have gone out of business. That's one more warning about relying on actively managed mutual funds as long-term investments.

In inefficient markets, the most successful managers may achieve unusually large returns. But common sense tells us that for each big success, there must also be a big failure.

While it is alleged that indexing doesn't work in markets that are less-efficient than the large stocks in the S&P 500, the impressive performance of the small- and mid-cap indexes suggest that it works perfectly well. *As it must.* For, whether markets are efficient or inefficient, as a group all investors in that segment earn the return of that segment. In inefficient markets, the most successful managers may achieve unusually large returns. But never forget that, as a group, all investors in any discrete segment of the stock market must be, and are, average. Common sense tells us that for each big success, there must also be a big failure. But after all those deductions of even larger management fees that funds incur in less efficient markets, and the damaging impact of their even larger turnover costs, the aggregate lag is even wider. So even in inefficient market segments, index funds, with their tiny costs, win again.

International funds are also subject to the same allegation that it is easier for managers to win in (supposedly) less-efficient markets. But also to no avail. S&P reports that the international index (world markets, less U.S. stocks) outpaced 80 percent of actively managed international equity funds over the past five years. Similarly, the S&P Emerging Markets Index outpaced 88 percent of emerging market funds. With indexing so successful in both more efficient and less efficient markets alike, and in U.S. markets and global markets, I'm not sure what additional data are required to close the case in favor of index funds.

But while investing in particular market sectors is done most efficiently through index funds, betting on the winning sectors is exactly that: betting. *But betting is a loser's game.* Why? Largely because emotions are almost certain to have a powerful negative impact on the returns that investors achieve. Whatever returns each sector may earn, the investors in those very sectors will likely, if not certainly, fall well behind them. For there is abundant evidence that the most popular sector funds of the day are those that have recently enjoyed the most spectacular recent performance. As a result, after-the-fact popularity is a recipe for unsuccessful investing.

**Indexing stock market sectors, a strong idea.
Betting on stock market sectors, a weak reality.**

For example, when Vanguard created the industry's first Growth Index Fund and Value Index Fund in 1992, the former was designed for younger investors who focused on wealth accumulation, were seeking tax-efficiency, and were willing to assume larger risks. The latter was designed for older investors who focused on wealth preservation, were seeking higher income, and were happy to reduce their risks. Alas, while the original idea was strong, the ensuing reality was weak. What followed their introduction was a classic example of performance chasing.

During the 1993 to 1997 period, the stock market was relatively placid, and value stocks and growth stocks delivered similar returns. Then in the new economy bubble, growth stocks took off, earning a cumulative return by 2000 that left value stocks in the dust (1992 to March 2000: Growth Index total return, 364 percent; Value Index total return, 229 percent). *Après moi le deluge!* Reversion to the mean took hold, and growth stocks plummeted through 2002.

Investor interest in the two fund styles was well balanced during the early years. But in the bubble that followed, investors poured $11 billion into the soaring Growth Index Fund, nearly four times the $3 billion invested in the sedate Value Index Fund. Then, in the aftermath, investors switched their loyalty, with net redemptions of $850 million in the Growth Index Fund during 2001 to 2006 and net purchases approaching $2 billion in the Value Index Fund.

Since 1993, the two funds have achieved substantial positive returns on the standard time-weighted basis—9.1 percent per year for Growth and 11.2 percent for Value. With their counterproductive timing and selection, however, investors in these index funds have not come even close to matching those returns. The average dollar-weighted return earned by investors in the Growth Index Fund was a pathetic 0.9 percent per year. While investors in the Value Index Fund did better, their return of 7.6 percent still lagged the return on the Value Index Fund by 3.6 percentage points per year.

Since 1993, the cumulative return of the Growth Index has been 224 percent, versus 320 percent for the Value Index, based on the traditional calculation of fund performance. The Growth Index Fund investor, meanwhile, earned but 13 percent, and the Value Index Fund investor earned about 170 percent. Despite my best intentions when they were formed, Vanguard's Growth Fund and Value Index Funds proved to be a paradigm for the ways that investors fool themselves, relinquishing perfectly acceptable long-term returns in their search to find the Holy Grail of extra returns in the short run.

So look before you leap in trying to pick which market sector to bet on. It may not be as exciting, but owning the classic stock market index fund is the ultimate strategy. It holds the mathematical certainty that marks it as the gold standard in investing, for try as they might, the alchemists of active management cannot turn their own lead, copper, or iron into gold. Just avoid complexity, rely on simplicity, take costs out of the equation and trust the arithmetic.

Don't Take My Word for It

You may think that I am too pessimistic in calculating the odds that only 2 percent of all equity mutual portfolios will outperform the stock market over 50 years. If so, consider the odds calculated by **Michael J. Mauboussin,** chief market strategist at Legg Mason, adjunct professor at Columbia Business School, and author of the best-selling *More than You Know.* While my 2 percent estimate would mean that 1 portfolio in 50 would outperform the stock market over 50 years, Mauboussin calculates the odds of a fund outperforming for 15 years consecutively at 1 in 223,000, and at 1 in 31 million over 21 years. Either way, the odds of outpacing an all-market index fund are, well, terrible.

Now listen to Warren Buffett's widely esteemed partner **Charlie Munger,** who eloquently states the case for shunning the foolish complexity of investing and opting for simplicity: "At large charitable foundations in recent years there has been a drift toward more complexity. In some endowment funds, there are not few but many investment counselors, chosen by an additional layer of consultants who are hired to decide which investment counselors are best, help in allocating

(continued)

funds to various categories, insure that claimed investment styles are scrupulously followed . . . [plus] a third layer of the security analysts employed by investment banks. There is one thing sure about all this complexity, the total cost of all the investment management, plus the frictional costs of fairly often getting in and out of many large investment positions, can easily reach 3 percent of foundation net worth per annum. All the equity investors, in total, will surely bear a performance disadvantage per annum equal to the total croupiers' costs they have jointly elected to bear. . . . And it is unescapable that exactly half of the investors will get a result below the median result after the croupier's take, a median result that may well be somewhere between unexciting and lousy. The wiser choice is to dispense with the consultants and reduce the investment turnover, by changing to indexed investment in equities." (Once again, shades of the Gotrocks family.)

Chapter Thirteen

Bond Funds and Money Market Funds

Where Those Relentless Rules Are Even More Powerful

So far, my discussion of the index fund (and its hand-maiden, low investment costs) has related to the stock market and to equity mutual funds. But the relentless rules of humble arithmetic with which I've regaled you also apply—arguably even more forcefully—to bond funds and money market funds.

Perhaps it's obvious why this is so. While a seemingly infinite number of factors influence the stock market and each individual stock that is traded there, a single factor influences the bond market and the money market (and for that matter, each individual fixed-income security) far more than any other: the prevailing level of interest rates. Managers of fixed-income funds can't do much, if anything, to influence rates. If they don't like the rates established in that market, calling the Treasury Department or the Federal Reserve, or otherwise trying to change the supply-and-demand equation, is unlikely to bear fruit.

So let's be clear: In the long run, virtually 100 percent of the return on any bond fund or money market fund is accounted for by the net interest income it generates for its shareholders. The only way for a manager to add an increment to that return is to make interest rate bets—for example, by selling bonds when he expects rates to go up (and prices down), and then buying bonds when the reverse is expected to happen. If you think that picking stocks and timing their purchase is hard, just imagine how hard it is to execute these same strategies successfully in the incredibly efficient precincts of the bond market.

Thus, managers of fixed income funds almost inevitably deliver a gross return that parallels the baseline constituted by the interest rate environment. Yes, a few managers might do better—even do better for a long time—by being extra smart, or extra lucky, or by taking extra risk. Yet even the best bond and money market managers can add only a few fractions of one percent per year to your long-term returns, albeit only by risking a comparable shortfall. What's more, even if they achieve these margins, they rarely overcome the fees, sales loads, and expenses involved in acquiring their services.

While these costs make the task of adding returns far more difficult, overly confident bond fund managers may be tempted to take just a little extra risk by extending maturities of the bonds in the portfolio. (Long-dated bonds—say, 30 years—are much more volatile than short-term bonds—say, two years—but usually provide higher yields.) They are also tempted to reduce the investment quality of the portfolio, holding less in U.S. Treasury bonds (rated AAA) or in investment-grade corporate bonds (rated BBB or better), and holding more in below-investment-grade bonds (BB or lower), or even some so-called junk bonds, rated below CC or even unrated.

Since stocks represent the residual ownership (or equity) of corporations, the word *safety* is not usually associated with them. Unlike bonds, stocks can't default. Bonds, on the other hand, represent debt. If the payments of interest that corporations and governments promise to make every six months are threatened, their ratings will be downgraded and the market value of their bonds reduced. And if they finally fail to make the promised payments, they enter bankruptcy proceedings. Where bonds are concerned, Brandeis's warning becomes particularly meaningful: "Remember, O stranger, arithmetic is the first of the sciences and the mother of safety."

There are too many types of bond funds to try your patience by examining all of them. So this chapter presents the three basic maturity levels that have become the industry standard, one in each of the three major bond segments—taxable (corporate and government) bonds, tax-exempt municipal bonds, and U.S. Treasury issues. The discussion begins with intermediate-term taxable bond funds; then turns to long-term tax-exempt bond funds; and finally evaluates funds investing in short-term U.S. Treasury notes.

Among intermediate-term taxable bond funds, the low-cost index fund is truly a superior performer.

As you'll see, the low-cost intermediate-term bond index fund is a truly superior performer* (Exhibit 13.1). (A finding that indexing wins should no longer surprise you.) With a 10-year return averaging 6.8 percent annually, it comes within a whisker of outpacing the (cost-adjusted) return of the comparable Lehman 5–10 Year

---

* I apologize, sort of, for using Vanguard funds for the examples of market indexes. But there are few other bond funds in these categories that implement index or index-like strategies, and literally none with lower costs for individual investors.

EXHIBIT 13.1   Intermediate-Term Taxable Bond Funds: Returns and Costs, 1996–2006

	Annual Return	Final Value (Initial Investment of $10,000)	Expense Ratio
Vanguard IT Bond Index Fund	6.79%	$19,289	0.18%
Lehman 5–10 Year Gov/Corp. Index[a]	6.90	19,488	0.20[a]
Average fund[b]	5.50	17,081	1.00

[a] Assumed annual expense ratio deducted.
[b] Includes both corporate and government funds.

Government/Corporate Bond Index. What is more, the index fund's annual return of 6.8 percent was almost 25 percent higher than the 5.5 percent return of its average peer. While the actively managed bond funds as a group earned a lower gross return than either the index fund or the index, relative cost proved to be the principal differentiator in net return.

As a group, the portfolios of the actively managed bond funds include about 25 percent corporate and 75 percent U.S. government bonds (largely bonds of government agencies), whereas the bond index and the bond index fund include about 50 percent in corporates and 50 percent in governments. While the bond index fund carried slightly more volatility risk (with an annualized standard deviation of 5 percent versus 3.7 percent for the active managers), both figures represent an extremely low risk level.

And so the message echoes. Among intermediate-term taxable bond funds, in terms of maximizing your return and minimizing your risk, the low-cost index fund is truly a superior performer. The Vanguard Intermediate-Term Bond Index Fund, for example, has an expense ratio of 0.18 percent, less than one-fifth of the 1.0 percent expense ratio of its average peer. In addition, its return benefits from the absence of sales loads. *Always avoid bond funds with sales loads.* (A typical 5 percent load would obliterate your entire yield for the first year.) With a cumulative final value of an initial investment of $10,000 growing to $19,289 in the index fund, versus just $17,081 for its average rival, the index strategy is a winning strategy, outpacing an amazing 550 of its 570 peers over the past decade.

Among long-term tax-exempt bond funds, once again, indexing wins.

Now let's consider long-term maturities, with a focus on tax-exempt municipal bond funds. Because of complexities in the construction of municipal bond indexes, there are no pure index funds in this category. But the results of the major index in the field (the

Lehman Brothers Tax-Exempt 10-Year Maturity Index)
confirm the power of indexing in surpassing the returns
provided by the average active bond manager (Exhibit
13.2). Since the index provided a gross return of 5.93
percent, a comparable index fund, after assumed costs
of 0.20 percent, would have provided a 5.73 percent net
annual return.

By way of comparison, the Vanguard Long-Term
Tax-Exempt Bond Fund—whose expense ratio of 0.15
percent is actually slightly below these assumed costs for
the index fund—provided a net return of 5.85 percent, a
bit higher than the assumed return of the bond index
fund. Like the index fund, this bond fund is broadly diversified, holds a high-quality portfolio (87 percent rated

**EXHIBIT 13.2   Long-Term Municipal Bond Funds:
Returns and Costs, 1996–2006**

	Annual Return	Final Value (Initial Investment of $10,000)	Expense Ratio
Vanguard Long-Term Munici-pal Bond Fund	5.85%	$17,657	0.15%
Lehman 10-Year Municipal Index*	5.73	17,458	0.20*
Average fund	5.01	16,306	1.03

* Assumed expense ratio deducted.

A or better, even higher than its actively managed peers), and minimizes turnover.

Once again, low costs lead to higher returns. The 5.73 percent annual return of the hypothetical municipal bond index fund was roughly 15 percent more than the 5.0 percent earned by the average long-term municipal fund, even though the actively managed funds were assuming higher risks—15 percent in lower-rated bonds versus 4 percent for the index and 13 percent for the Vanguard fund.

Over the past decade, $10,000 initially invested in the Vanguard Long-Term Municipal Bond Fund grew to $17,657, versus $16,306 for its average rival. With low-costs, broad diversification, and no serious attempt to outguess the market in long-term tax-exempt bond funds, once again indexing wins. Its close proxy, the Vanguard Long-Term Municipal Bond Fund, ranked first among its 194 peers.

--------------------------- ∼ ---------------------------

Among short-term Treasury funds, the lowest cost option wins again.

Our sweep of the bond fund arena concludes with an examination of short-term funds investing in U.S. Treasury obligations (Exhibit 13.3). There are few surprises here. The net return earned by the index itself (5.06 percent per year, adjusted for an assumed expense ratio of

EXHIBIT 13.3   Short-Term Treasury Bond Funds: Returns and Costs, 1996–2006

	Annual Return	Final Value (Initial Investment of $10,000)	Expense Ratio
Vanguard Short-Term Bond Index	5.06%	$16,382	0.16%
Lehman 1–5 Government Fund	5.06	16,382	0.20*
Average fund	4.54	15,588	0.92

* Assumed expense ratio deducted.

0.20 percent) outpaces the average fund. Again, while the Vanguard Short-Term Government Bond Fund is not, technically speaking, an index fund, it tracks the index return with remarkable precision, turning in a net average annual return of 5.06 percent over the past decade. The lowest cost options win again, outpacing 97 of the 122 short-term government funds. (Treasurys being Treasurys, investment quality is virtually uniform. Both the Vanguard index fund and the index itself hold 100 percent of their portfolios in short-term U.S. Treasury notes, and the active funds hold 99 percent.)

With its towering 0.92 percent average expense ratio, the average short-term bond fund has a lot to overcome. It doesn't succeed—it can't succeed—in overcoming that handicap, even by assuming somewhat more volatility risk than the government index and the Vanguard, both of which funds displayed slightly less volatility than their active peers. (Again, many of these actively managed funds carry sales charges, averaging 3 percent, which are incorporated into the returns shown in Exhibit 13.3.)

The tracking of its benchmark, its quality parity, and its extremely low expenses mark the Vanguard Short-Term Treasury Bond Fund as the functional equivalent of the Lehman 1–5 Year Government Bond Index. While there are no bond funds that track this index, the Vanguard fund is the virtual equivalent of an index fund. Both provided cumulative gains on an initial investment of $10,000 of an identical $16,382 over the past decade, compared with $15,588 for the average short-term Treasury fund.

— ∿ —

Among money market funds—surprise! —low cost wins again.

Money market funds can be thought of as very short-term bond funds with uniformly high credit quality. Federal regulations limit money market funds to high-grade commercial and bank paper, and as a practical matter limit maturities to a very short term (about 60 days), to maintain a stable asset value of $1.00 per share. (Unlike bank savings accounts, money market funds are not guaranteed by the Federal Deposit Insurance Corporation.) As a result, money market funds hold portfolios with generally similar quality (though a bit of "stretching" for yield often goes on) and very short maturity (usually averaging about 40 days). As a result, they tend to earn substantially identical gross yields on their portfolios.

With their short maturities, extremely high credit quality, and broadly diversified portfolios, money market funds essentially become commodities. Thus, when all else is equal (as it is here), relative performance is determined by relative cost. So, even more than in stock index funds and bond index funds, cost tells virtually the entire story in money market funds.

If we rank the records of all 190 money market funds in terms of the returns they have delivered to investors over the past 10 years (highest first) and then compare their expense ratio (lowest first), the relationship is almost perfect. Exhibit 13.4 echoes the cost versus return analysis of Exhibits 13.1 to 13.3. The Vanguard Prime Money Market Fund, close cousin to our hypothetical index fund, was among the leaders, producing a net annual return of 3.77 percent for the past decade, some 15 percent above the return on the average money market fund. Cumulatively, a $10,000 initial investment in the Vanguard Prime Money Market Fund grew to $14,478 over the

EXHIBIT 13.4   Money Market Funds: Returns, Costs, and Risks, 1996–2006

	Gross Return	Expense Ratio	Net Return	Final Value (Investment of $10,000)
Vanguard Prime Money Market Fund	4.07%	0.30%	3.77%	$14,478
A1/P1 Commercial Paper Index*	4.07	0.20*	3.87	14,618
Average Prime Money Market Fund	4.05	0.82	3.25	13,785

* Estimated return and expense ratio on a hypothetical index fund.

past decade, versus $13,785 for its average peer. Among 190 comparable funds, it ranked number 7.

Remarkably, while the data are not shown in Exhibit 13.4, money market funds in the high-cost quartile earned a gross return of 4.10 percent (about equal to the average). But with a shocking annual expense ratio of 1.39 percent, these high-cost funds delivered a net return of just 2.71 percent to their owners. Why would investors pay more than a 0.50 percent annual cost for a money market fund? The answer is beyond me. (They should probably have their heads examined.) How the supposedly independent directors of these 45 money funds with expense ratios at or above the 1.00 percent level could vote to approve such fees is an even bigger question. Their job is to represent the interests of the fund shareholders, and they have failed. But intelligent investors don't need to fail. If you avoid these high-cost money market funds in favor of low-cost funds, you inevitably earn superior returns.

* * *

Summing up, I realize full well that investors are far more focused on equity funds and the stock market than on fixed-income funds. Nonetheless, smart investors will save themselves lots of money—and substantially improve their returns—if they apply the same principles of broad diversification, low-cost, no-load, minimal turnover, and long-term investing when they select fixed income funds. These are the very commonsense characteristics that enable index funds to guarantee your fair share of the returns in the bond and money markets, even as they do in all financial markets.

Don't Take My Word for It

While not a lot has been written about the remarkable (and remarkably obvious) value of index funds that invest in bonds, the convictions expressed in this chapter have been strongly reinforced by **Walter R. Good,** CFA and **Roy W. Hermansen,** CFA, in *Index Your Way to Investment Success.* "Comparison of expenses, transaction costs, and, where applicable, sales loads identify the cost advantage for bond index funds. For the purposes of projecting returns, let's assume

(continued)

that the actively managed fund and the benchmark index fund each hold bonds that, overall, yield the same 7 percent annual rate of return. For the actively-managed load funds, the index fund advantage amounts to 1.2 percentage points per year. The data provide a sobering glimpse of the challenge encountered by the active bond fund manager . . . and suggest how much additional return active management may have to add—on average over an extended period—just to break even! . . . Near-index bond mutual funds provide an alternative to indexing the bond market. While the funds do not completely conform to the index fund model, they share key characteristics: very high degree of diversification [in the specified market segment], very low expense ratio, very low transaction costs, and absence of sales loads."

Once again, further confirmation comes from across the pond. England's **Timothy Hale,** author of *Smarter Investing—Simpler Decisions for Better Results*, writes, "You should not overlook the efficacy of index investing for bonds, which up to now has been whispered rather than shouted from the rooftops. The evidence is compelling and comes down firmly in favor of investing in index funds. . . . Over the ten-year period 1988–1998, US bond index funds returned 8.9 per cent a year against 8.2 per cent for actively managed bond funds (with) index funds beating 85 per cent of all active funds. This differential is largely due to fees."

Chapter Fourteen

Index Funds
That Promise to Beat
the Market

The New Paradigm?

SINCE THE INCEPTION OF the first index mutual fund in 1975, indexing—investing in passively managed, broadly diversified, low-cost, stock and bond index funds—has proved to be both a remarkable artistic success and a remarkable commercial success. In previous chapters, we've evaluated the success of index funds in providing returns to investors that have vastly surpassed the returns achieved by investors in actively managed mutual funds.

Given that artistic success, the commercial success of indexing is hardly surprising. Today, most indexed assets are concentrated in classic index funds representing the broad U.S. stock market (the S&P 500 or the Dow Jones Wilshire 5000) the broad international stock market (the Morgan Stanley EAFE [Europe, Australia, and Far East] Index); and the broad U.S. bond market. Assets of these traditional classic stock index funds have grown from $16 million in 1976 to $445 million in 1986, to $68 billion in 1996, to $369 billion in 2006—7 percent of the assets of all equity mutual funds. Assets of bond index funds have also soared—from $132 million in 1986, to $6 billion in 1996, to $62 billion in 2006—7 percent of the assets of all taxable bond funds.

Indexing has become a competitive field. The largest managers of the classic index funds are engaged in a fiercely competitive price war, cutting their expense ratios to draw the assets of investors who are smart enough to realize the price is the difference. This trend is great for index fund investors. But it slashes profits to index fund managers and discourages entrepreneurs who start new fund ventures in the hopes of enriching themselves by building fund empires.

So how can promoters take advantage of the proven attributes that underlie the success of the traditional index fund? Why, create new indexes! Then claim that they will consistently outpace the broad market indexes that up until now have pretty much defined how we think of indexing. And then charge a higher fee for that higher potential reward, whether or not it is ever actually delivered.

Traditional indexes, as noted in Chapter 3, are *cap-weighted*. That is, the weight of each stock (or bond) in the index portfolio is determined by its market capitalization. The total U.S. stock market, with a value of $15 trillion, represents the collective investment of all stockholders of U.S. equities. So it follows that, together, all investors as a group earn precisely the market's return. (Remember the Gotrocks family, in Chapter 1.)

If the market rises by 10 percent, all investors as a group earn 10 percent (before costs). So the miracle, as it were, of the index fund, is simple arithmetic. By minimizing all those costs of investing, it guarantees that its participants will earn higher net returns than all the other participants in stock ownership as a group. This is the *only* approach to equity investing that can guarantee such an outcome.

The only way to beat the market portfolio is to depart from the market portfolio.

The only way to beat the market portfolio is to depart from the market portfolio. And this is what active managers strive to do, individually. But collectively, they can't succeed. For their trading merely shifts ownership from one holder to another. All that swapping of stock certificates back and forth, however it may work out for a given buyer or seller, enriches only our financial intermediaries.

The active money manager, in effect, puts forth this argument. "I'm smarter than the others in the market. I can discover undervalued stocks, and when the market discovers them and they rise in price I'll sell them. Then I'll discover other undervalued stocks and repeat the process all over again. I know that the stock market is highly efficient, but through my intelligence, my expert analysts, my computer programs, and my trading strategies, I can spot temporary inefficiencies and capture them, over and over again."

As we have seen in Chapter 8, some fund managers have actually succeeded in this task. But they are precious few in number—over the past 36 years, just three funds out of 355—$^8/_{10}$ of 1 percent—have consistently distinguished themselves. Nonetheless, hope springs eternal among money managers, and they strive for excellence. Of course, they believe in themselves. (This field has few shrinking violets!) But they also have a vested financial interest in persuading investors that if they have done well in the past they will continue to do so in the future. And if they haven't done well in the past, well, better days are always ahead.

In recent years, something new has been added to the mix. There are now financial entrepreneurs who believe, I'm sure, sincerely (if with a heavy dollop of self-interest), that they can create indexes that will beat the market. Interesting! They have developed new methods of weighting portfolio holdings that they vow will outperform the traditional market-cap-weighted portfolio that represents the holdings of investors as a group.

This new breed of indexers—not, in fact, indexers, but active strategists—focuses on weighting portfolios by so-called fundamental factors. Rather than weighting by market cap, they use a combination of factors such as corporate revenues, cash flows, profits, or dividends (for example, the portfolio may be weighted by the dollar amount of dividends distributed by each corporation, rather than the dollar amount of its market capitalization). They argue, fairly enough, that in a cap-weighted portfolio, half of the stocks are overvalued to a greater or lesser extent, and half are undervalued.

——————————————— ∽ ———————————————

**No one would have the temerity to promote a
new strategy that has lagged in the past.**

———————————————————————————————

The traditional indexer responds: "Of course. But who really knows which half is which?" The new fundamental indexers unabashedly answer, "We do." They actually claim to know which is which. And—this will not surprise you—the fundamental factors they have identified as the basis for their portfolio selections actually have outpaced the traditional indexes in the past. (We call this *data mining*. For you can be sure that no one would have the temerity to promote a new strategy that has lagged the traditional index fund in the past.)

The members of this new breed are not shy about their prescience. They claim variously, if a tad grandiosely, that they represent a "new wave" in indexing, a "revolution" that will offer investors better returns and lower volatility, and a "new paradigm." Indeed, they describe themselves as the new Copernicans, after the man who concluded that the center of the solar system was not the earth, but the sun. They compare the traditional market-cap weighted indexers with ancient astronomers who attempted to perpetuate the Ptolemaic view of an earth-centered universe. And they assure the world that we're at the brink of a "huge paradigm shift" in indexing.

They come armed with vast statistical studies that prove how well their methodologies have worked in the past (or at least since 1962, when their back-tested studies began). But think for a moment about the message of Chapter 8: in mutual fund investing, *the past is not prologue*. These new paradigmists casually ignore that truism.

For example: "Dividend indexes outperform capitalized-weighted indexes." (Not, "have outperformed in the past.") "The fundamental index adds more than twice as much incremental return." (Not, "has added in the past.")

Investors (and managers, too) love to believe that the past is prologue. It would make life so easy. But it is no accident that these new index funds are being introduced only after their strategies have seen their best days. Following the stock market bubble burst in 2000, value stocks outpaced growth stocks (the market-cap index holds both) over the subsequent five years; and for dividend-paying stocks, the pattern is about the same.

Even including this recent advantage, the long-term margins of superiority achieved by these theoretically constructed back-tested portfolios are not large—between 1 percent and 2 percent per year. How much of that edge would have been confiscated by their expense ratios? (The lowest is 0.28 percent; the average is about 0.50 percent; the highest that I've seen is 1.89 percent.) How much would have been confiscated by their extra portfolio turnover costs compared with the classic index funds? How much would have been confiscated by extra taxes paid by shareholders when that turnover resulted in gains? Even if the modest margins claimed in the past were to repeat—which, I believe, is highly unlikely—these back-tested hypothetical returns would be significantly eroded, if not totally erased, by those costs.

---------------------- ∽ ----------------------

If these paradigms actually have been right in the past, won't they therefore be wrong in the future?

But the central issue remains: how can one claim that the past will be prologue without a scintilla of apparent doubt? The new paradigmists have never explained why these fundamental factors have been systematically underpriced by the market in the past. And, if they have been underpriced, why investors, hungry to capitalize on that apparent past inefficiency, won't bid up prices until the undervaluation no longer remains. Put another way, if these promoters of the purported new paradigms actually have been right in the past, won't they therefore be wrong in the future?

When active managers of equity funds claim to have a way of uncovering extra value in our highly (but not perfectly) efficient U.S. stock market, investors will look at their past record, consider the manager's strategies, and invest or not. These new index managers are in fact active managers. But they not only claim prescience, but a prescience that gives them confidence that certain sectors of the market (such as dividend-paying stocks) will remain undervalued as far ahead as the eye can see.

I recommend skepticism. I have always been impressed by the inexorable tendency for reversion to the mean in security returns. For example, mutual funds with a value mandate have generally outperformed those with a growth mandate since the late 1960s. But since 1977—indeed since 1937—there has been little to choose between the two. In fact, from 1937 through 1967, growth mutual funds rather consistently trumped value mutual funds. Never think you know more than the market. Nobody does.

We never know when that reversion to the mean will come to the various sectors of the stock market. But we do know that such changes in style leadership have invariably occurred in the past. With so much of the stock market's volatility based on expectations (emotions) rather than business (economics), what else could we expect? Before we too easily accept that fundamental indexing— relying on style tilts toward dividends, value, or smallness—is the new paradigm, we need a longer sense of history. We also need to call on our own common sense that warns us that hindsight plays tricks on our minds.

There have been many new paradigms over the years. None has persisted. The "concept" stocks of the Go-Go years in the 1960s came and went. So did the "Nifty Fifty" era that soon followed. The "January effect" of small-cap superiority came and went. Option-income funds and "Government plus" funds came and went. In the late 1990s, high-tech stocks and "new economy" funds came and went as well. Today, the asset values of the survivors remain far below their peaks. Intelligent investors should approach with extreme caution a claim that any new paradigm is here to stay. That's not the way financial markets work.

∽

"The greatest enemy of a good plan is the dream of a perfect plan." Stick to the good plan.

Traditional all-market-cap-weighted index funds guarantee that you will receive your fair share of stock market returns, and virtually assure that you will outperform, over the long term, 90 percent or more of the other investors in the marketplace. Maybe this new paradigm of fundamental indexing—unlike all the other new paradigms I've seen—will work. But maybe it won't. I urge investors not to be tempted by the siren song of paradigms that promise the accumulation of wealth that will be far beyond the rewards of the classic index fund. Don't forget the prophetic warning of Carl von Clausewitz, military theorist and Prussian general of the early nineteenth century, *"The greatest enemy of a good plan is the dream of a perfect plan."* Put your dreaming away, pull out your common sense, and stick to the good plan represented by the classic index fund.

Don't Take My Word for It

While I feel strongly on this point, I am not alone. First hear these words from **Gregory Mankiw,** Harvard professor and former chairman of the President's Council of Economic Advisers. "I am placing my bets with Bogle on this one." Then listen to **William Sharpe,** professor of finance at Stanford and Nobel Laureate in Economics: "It is quite remarkable that people think that somehow a scheme that weights stocks differently than capitalization can dominate a capitalization-weighted index. . . . New paradigms come and go. Betting against the market (and spending a considerable amount of money to do so) is indeed likely to be a hazardous undertaking."

Consider, too, this caution from **John R. Minahan,** director of research at New England Pension Consultants: "I am amazed by all the managers that make an assertion of the type: 'In the long run X always wins,' where X could be dividend yield, earnings growth, quality of management, a quantitative factor or mix of factors, etc.—yet are unable cite a reason why X should be systematically underpriced by the market. The managers may be able to point to data suggesting that X has been associated with excess returns in the past, but without a plausible explanation

(continued)

of *why* X should outperform. Such data do not convince me that X is likely to outperform in the future."

Finally, consider this affirmation of classic indexing from Wharton School Professor **Jeremy J. Siegel,** author of *Stocks for the Long Run* and adviser to WisdomTree Investments, the promoter of the dividend-driven fundamental model. "It can be shown that maximum diversification is achieved by holding each stock *in proportion to its value to the entire market* (italics added). . . . Hindsight plays tricks on our minds . . . often distorts the past and encourages us to play hunches and outguess other investors, who in turn are playing the same game. For most of us, trying to beat the market leads to disastrous results . . . our actions lead to much lower returns than can be achieved by just staying in the market . . . matching the market year after year with index funds (such as) the Vanguard 500 Portfolio . . . and Vanguard's Total Stock Market Index Fund." (This quotation is from the first edition of Dr. Siegel's book in 1994. I understand that he has every right to change his mind.)

Chapter Fifteen

The Exchange Traded Fund

A Trader to the Cause

EVEN BEFORE THE RISE of the so-called new paradigm of fundamental indexing described in Chapter 14, traditional indexing was being challenged by a sort of wolf-in-sheep's clothing, the exchange traded fund (ETF). Simply put, the ETF is a fund designed to facilitate trading in its shares, dressed in the guise of the traditional index fund.

If long-term investing was the original paradigm for the classic index fund designed 31 years ago, surely using index funds as trading vehicles can only be described as short-term speculation. If the broadest possible diversification was the original paradigm, surely holding discrete—even widely-diversified—sectors of the market offers less diversification and commensurately more risk. If the original paradigm was minimal cost, then holding market sector index funds that are themselves low-cost obviates neither the brokerage commissions entailed in trading them nor the tax burdens incurred if one has the good fortune to do so successfully.

———————— ∿ ————————

Typical ETF investors have absolutely no idea what relationship their investment return will have to the return earned by the stock market.

As to the quintessential aspect of the original paradigm—assuring, indeed guaranteeing, that investors will earn their fair share of the stock market's return—the fact is that investors who trade ETFs have nothing even resembling such a guarantee. In fact, after all the selection challenges, the timing risks, the extra costs, and the added taxes—typical ETF investors have absolutely no idea what relationship their investment return will have to the return earned by the stock market.

These differences between the *classic* index fund and the index fund *nouveau* represented by the ETF are stark (Exhibit 15.1). Exchange traded funds march to a different

EXHIBIT 15.1   Classic Index Funds versus Index Funds Nouveau

| | Classic Index Funds | Exchange Traded Funds | | |
| | | Broad Index | | Specialized Index |
		Investing	Trading	
Broadest possible diversification	Yes	Yes	Yes	No
Longest time horizon	Yes	Yes	No	Rarely
Lowest possible cost	Yes	Yes	No*	No*
Greatest possible tax efficiency	Yes	Yes	No	No
Highest possible share of market return	Yes	Yes	Unknown	Unknown

* Including trading costs.

tune than the original, and I'm left to wonder, in the words of the old song, "What have they done to my song, ma?"

The first exchange traded fund, created in 1992 by Nathan Most, was named "Standard & Poor's Depositary Receipts" (SPDRs), and quickly dubbed "Spider." It was a brilliant idea. Investing in the S&P 500 Index, operated at low cost with high tax efficiency, and held for the long term, it held the prospect of providing ferocious competition to the traditional S&P 500 Index Fund. (Brokerage commissions, however, made it less suitable for investors making small investments regularly.) Most of the investors in the Spiders, however, were not long-term investors. They were active money managers, hedgers, and professional traders. Currently, some 65 million (!) shares of Spiders ($8.8 billion worth) are now traded every *day*.

From that single fund, ETFs have grown to be a huge part—$410 billion—of the $1 trillion index fund asset base, a 41 percent share, up from just 9 percent as 2000 began and only 3 percent a decade ago. Led by index portfolios whose shares are rapidly traded in narrow market segments (despite their stark contradiction of each of the five concepts underlying the original index fund), ETFs have become a force to be reckoned with in the financial markets. Their amazing growth certainly says something about the energy of Wall Street's financial entrepreneurs, the focus of money managers on gathering assets, the marketing power of brokerage firms, and the willingness—nay, eagerness—of investors to favor complexity over simplicity, continuing to believe, against all odds, that they can beat the market.

The growth of ETFs has approached a stampede, not only in number but in diversity. There are now nearly 340 ETFs available, including 122 already formed during 2006, and the range of the investment choices available is remarkable.* There are 12 total stock market index funds (U.S. and international) such as the Spider, still the largest segment in terms of assets; 68 focused on investment styles; 173 based on stock market sectors; and 58 concentrating their assets in particular foreign countries. There

---

* Early in 2007, 343 ETFs were on the drawing board, soon to be launched. This stampede suggests a new investment fad. Such fads have rarely enhanced the well-being of investors.

are also a handful of bond ETFs and a scattering of ETFs utilizing high leverage (doubling the swings in the stock market), tracking commodity prices and currencies, and using other high-risk strategies.

The march of assets into ETFs has also been impressive. Since 1999, ETFs have drawn $280 billion of net new money, even larger than the $190 billion flowing into their classic cousins. What's more, the flow into style, sector, and foreign funds has overwhelmed the flow into the broad stock market index component. While these broad funds accounted for 100 percent of the total ETF inflow in the early years, they accounted for less than 20 percent from 2000 through 2006.

— ✍ —

The renowned Purdey shotgun is great for big-game hunting in Africa. But it's also excellent for suicide.

All-stock-market ETFs are the only instance in which an ETF can replicate, and possibly even improve on, the five paradigms of the original index fund listed earlier. *But only when they are bought and held for the long-term.* Their annual expense ratios are usually—but not always—slightly lower than their mutual fund counterparts, although commissions on purchases erode any advantage, and may even overwhelm it. While their tax efficiency should be higher, actual practice so far has failed to confirm theory, and investors who trade them are subject to their own taxes. Their use by long-term investors is minimal. The Spiders are, in fact, marketed to day traders. As the advertisements say, *"Now you can trade the S&P 500 all day long, in real time."* I can't help likening the ETF—a cleverly designed financial instrument—to the renowned Purdey shotgun, supposedly the world's best. It's great for big-game hunting in Africa. But it's also excellent for suicide.

I suspect that too many ETFs will prove, if not suicidal to their owners in financial terms, at least wealth-depleting. We know that ETFs are largely used by traders, for the turnover of Spider shares is running at 3600 percent annual rate. The turnover for the NASDAQ Qubes is even higher, at 6,000 percent per year. It is only guesswork, but long-term investors hold perhaps 20 percent of the $100 billion assets of these Spider-like broadly diversified ETFs, or about $20 billion. The remaining assets, I presume, are held by market makers and arbitrageurs, making heavy use of short-selling and hedging strategies.

Assets of the other types of ETFs now total $310 billion. Trading these funds is also remarkably high. The shares of the major sector ETFs are typically turned over at an average annual rate of some 200 percent per year (an average holding period of just six months), with the most popular ETFs recently running turnover rates from 578 percent to

735 percent, all the way up to 7,100 percent (Russell 2000 iShares) and 8,500 percent (SPDR Energy shares). Could there be speculation going on here? In all, some $390 billion of the current $410 billion ETF base represents a vast departure from the beneficial attributes of the original index fund.

Yes, these specialized ETFs are diversified, but only in their narrow arenas. Owning the semiconductor industry is not diversification in any usual sense, nor is owning the South Korean stock market. And while sector ETFs frequently have the lowest expense ratios in their fields, they can run three to six times the level of the lowest-cost all-market index funds. What is more, sector ETFs not only carry brokerage and trading costs, but often are sold as parts of actively managed fund portfolios with adviser fees of 1 percent or more, or in wrap accounts with annual fees of 1.5 percent to 2.0 percent or more.

The net result of these differences is that sector ETFs as a group are virtually certain to earn returns that fall well short of the returns delivered by the stock market. Perhaps 1 percent to 3 percent a year is a fair estimate of these all-in costs, many times the 10 to 20 basis-point cost of the best classic index funds. It is not a trivial difference. For no matter how often derided or ignored, the tautology remains that sector funds, soundly administered, will earn a net return equal to the gross return of that sector, less intermediation costs.

But whatever returns each sector ETF may earn, the investors in those very ETFs will likely, if not certainly, earn returns that fall well behind them. There is abundant evidence that the most popular sector funds of the day are those that have recently enjoyed the most spectacular recent performance, and that such "after-the-fact" popularity is a recipe for unsuccessful investing. The lesson in Chapter 5—that mutual fund investors almost always do significantly worse than the funds they own, and still worse when they choose funds that are less diversified—is likely to be repeated in ETFs.

To illustrate this point, consider the record of the 20 best performing ETFs during 2003–2006. Only one earned a better return for its shareholders than the return it reported. The average shortfall in shareholder return was equal to 5 percentage points per year. The largest gap was 14 percentage points; iShares Austria reported a 42 percent return, but its investors earned just 28 percent. "Handle with Care" should be the first warning on the ETF label (though I have yet to see it used). Or perhaps: "CAUTION: PERFORMANCE CHASING AT WORK."

A "double whammy": betting on hot sectors (emotions) and paying heavy costs (expenses) are sure to be hazardous to your wealth.

And so we have a "double whammy": the near-inevitability of counterproductive market timing (emotions), as investors bet on sectors as they grow hot—and bet against them when they grow cold—combined with those heavy commissions and fees (expenses). Together, these two enemies of the equity investor are sure to be hazardous to your wealth, to say nothing of consuming giant globs of your time that could easily be used in more productive and enjoyable ways.

In 2006, ETFs were also at the cutting edge of the "market-beating" (at least in retrospect) strategies described earlier. These promoters and entrepreneurs seem to acknowledge that their "fundamental indexing" approach is a long-term strategy. Yet by choosing the ETF format, they strongly imply that bringing stockbrokers into the distribution mix and actively buying and selling the funds will lead to even larger short-term profits. I doubt it.

**ETFs are an entrepreneur's dream come true.
But are they an investor's dream come true?**

ETFs are clearly a dream come true for entrepreneurs, stock brokers, and fund managers. But is it too much to ask whether these index funds nouveau are an investor's dream come true? Do investors really benefit from being able to trade ETFs "all day long, in real time"? Is less diversification better than more diversification? Is trend-following a winner's game, or a loser's game? Are ETFs truly low-cost when we add brokerage commissions to their expense ratios? Is buy-and-sell (often with great frequency) really a better strategy than buy-and-hold? If the classic index fund was designed to capitalize on the wisdom of long-term investing, aren't investors in these index funds *nouveau* too often engaging in the folly of short-term speculation? Doesn't your own common sense give you the obvious answers to these questions?

On the broad spectrum that lies between advancing the interests of the business and the interests of the clients, where do ETFs fit? If you are making a single large initial purchase of either of those two versions of classic indexing—the Spider or the Vanguard Total Stock Market ETF—at a low commission rate and holding them for the long term, you'll profit from their low expense ratios and may even enjoy a bit of extra tax efficiency. But if you trade them, you're defying the relentless rules of humble arithmetic that are the key to successful investing. If you like the idea of sector ETFs, use the appropriate ones, don't trade them, and use them in the right way— sparingly, and only to diversify your portfolio.

Let me now answer the question I asked at the outset of this chapter, "What have they done to my song, ma?" As the creator of the world's first index fund all those years ago, I can only answer: "They've tied it up in a plastic bag and turned it upside down, ma, that's what they've done to my song." In short, the ETF is a *trader to the cause* of classic indexing. I urge intelligent investors to stay the course with the proven strategy. While I can't say that classic indexing is the *best* strategy ever devised, your common sense should reassure you that the number of strategies that are worse is infinite.

Don't Take My Word for It

In an essay entitled "Indexing Goes Hollywood," here's what **Don Phillips,** managing director of Morningstar, has said: "[T]here is a dark side to indexing that investors should not ignore. The potential for harm to investors increases as index offerings become more specialized, which is exactly what has happened in the world of ETFs. . . . In the right hands, precision tools can create great things; in the wrong ones, however, they can do considerable damage. In creating more complex offerings, the index community has found new revenue sources from . . . very specialized tools, but it has done so at the risk of doing considerable harm to less sophisticated investors. The test of character facing the index community is whether it ignores that risk or steps up and tries to mitigate it. The continued good name of indexing lies in the balance."

(continued)

From **Jim Wiandt,** editor of the *Journal of Indexes:* "I have always found it ironic that indexing—like most everything else in the world of finance—comes in waves. Hedge fund indexes, microcap indexes, dividend indexes, commodities indexes, China indexes and 'enhanced' indexes are all flavors of the month. And I'll give you three guesses as to what all these indexes have in common: (1) chasing returns, (2) chasing returns, or (3) chasing returns.

"If you believe in indexing, then you know that there is no free money. Ultimately, the push toward enhanced indexing is about enhancing the bottom line for managers. . . . But it's important for us to keep our eyes on the ball and remember what makes indexing, well, indexing. Low fees, broad diversification, hold hold hold. Don't believe the hype. Try to beat the market—in any manner—and you're likely to get beat . . . by about the cost of doing it."

And now listen carefully to the warnings from two senior officers of a major ETF sponsor. **Chief executive:** "For most people, sector funds don't make a lot of sense . . . [don't] stray too far from the market's course." **Chief investment officer:** "It would be unfortunate if people focused pin-point bets on very narrowly defined ETFs. These still involve nearly as much risk as concentrating on individual stock picks. . . . You're taking extraordinary risk. It's possible to take a good thing too far. . . . *How many people really need them?*"

Chapter Sixteen

What Would Benjamin Graham Have Thought about Indexing?

A Confirmation from Mr. Buffett

THE FIRST EDITION OF *The Intelligent Investor* was published in 1949. It was written by Benjamin Graham, the most respected money manager of the era, and coauthor (with David Dodd) of *Security Analysis,* a scholarly tome originally published in 1934. *The Intelligent Investor* is regarded as the best book of its kind—comprehensive, analytical, perceptive, and forthright—a book for the ages.

Although Benjamin Graham is best known by far for his focus on the kind of value investing represented by the category of stocks he describes as "bargain issues," he cautioned, "the aggressive investor must have a considerable knowledge of security values—enough, in fact, to warrant viewing his security operations as equivalent to a business enterprise. . . . It follows from this reasoning that *the majority of security owners should elect the defensive classification.*"

The majority of investors should be satisfied with the reasonably good return obtainable from a defensive portfolio.

Why? Because "[the majority of investors] do not have the time, or the determination, or the mental equipment to embark upon such investing as a quasi-business. They should therefore be satisfied with the reasonably good return obtainable from a defensive portfolio, and they should stoutly resist the recurrent temptation to increase this return by deviating into other paths." While the index fund was not even imagined in 1949, he was certainly describing the very approach that this precedent-setting fund would later follow. (Coincidently, it was also in 1949 that an article in *Fortune* magazine introduced me to the mutual fund industry, inspiring me to write my 1951 Princeton senior thesis on mutual funds, in which I even hinted at the index fund idea: "Mutual funds can make no claim to superiority over the market averages.")

For the defensive investor who required assistance, Graham originally recommended professional investment advisers who rely on "normal investment experience for their results . . . and who make no claim to being brilliant (but) pride themselves on being careful, conservative, and competent . . . whose chief value to their clients is in shielding them from costly mistakes." He cautioned about expecting too much from stock-exchange houses, arguing that "the Wall Street business fraternity . . . is still feeling its way toward the high standards and standing of a profession." (A half-century later, the quest remains far from complete.)

He also noted, profoundly if obviously, that Wall Street is "in business to make commissions, and that the way to succeed in business is to give customers what they want, trying hard to make money in a field where they are condemned almost by mathematical law to lose." Later on, in 1976, Graham described his opinion of Wall Street as, "highly unfavorable . . . a Falstaffian joke that frequently degenerates into a madhouse . . . a huge laundry in which institutions take in large blocks of each other's washing." (Shades of Harvard's Jack Meyer and Yale's David Swensen, from whom we heard earlier.)

In that first edition of *The Intelligent Investor,* Graham commended the use by investors of leading investment funds as an alternative to creating their own portfolios. Graham described the well-established mutual funds of his era as "competently managed, making fewer mistakes than the typical small investor," carrying a reasonable expense, and performing a sound function by acquiring and holding an adequately diversified list of common stocks.

But he was bluntly realistic about what fund managers might accomplish. He illustrated this point in his book with data showing that from 1937 through 1947, when the Standard & Poor's 500 Index provided a total return of 57 percent, the average mutual fund produced a total return of 54 percent, excluding the oppressive impact of sales loads. *(The more things change, the more they remain the same.)* Graham's conclusion: "The figures are not very impressive in *either* direction . . . on the whole, the managerial ability of invested funds has been just about able to absorb the expense burden and the drag of uninvested cash." In 1949, fund expenses and turnover costs were far lower than in the modern fund industry. That change explains why, as fund returns were overwhelmed by these costs in recent decades, the figures were impressive only in a negative direction.

By 1965, Graham's confidence that funds would produce the market's return, less costs, was somewhat shaken. "Unsoundly managed funds," he noted in a later edition of *The Intelligent Investor,* "can produce spectacular but largely illusionary profits for a while, followed inevitably by calamitous losses." He was describing the so-called performance funds of the mid-1960s Go-Go era, in which a "new breed that had a spectacular knack for coming up with winners . . . (managed by) bright, energetic, young people who promised to perform miracles with other people's money . . . (but) who have inevitably brought losses to their public in the end." He could have as easily been presciently describing the hundreds of risky "new economy" mutual funds formed during the great bull market of 1998 to 2000, and their utter collapse in the subsequent 50 percent market crash that followed.

~

"Unsoundly managed funds can produce spectacular but largely illusionary profits for a while, followed inevitably by calamitous losses."

Graham also would have been appalled, not only by the enormous (100 percent-plus) increase in those once-reasonable fund expenses, but also by the incredible increase in stock trading in mutual fund portfolios. During Graham's era, portfolio turnover ran to about 15 percent per year. It now averages more than 100 percent. Graham would surely, and accurately, have described such an approach as rank speculation that flies directly in the face of his deeply held investment principles.

Graham's timeless lesson for the intelligent investor, as valid today as when he prescribed it in his first edition, is clear: "the real money in investment will have to be made—as most of it has been made in the past—*not out of buying and selling but of owning and holding securities,* receiving interest and dividends and increases in value." His philosophy has been reflected over and over again in this book, exemplified in the parable of the Gotrocks family in Chapter 1 and the distinction between the business market and the expectations market in Chapter 2.

The real money in investment will be made not out of buying and selling but of owning and holding securities.

Owning and holding a diversified list of securities? Wouldn't Graham recommend a fund that essentially buys the entire stock market and holds it forever, patiently receiving interest and dividends and increases in value? Doesn't his admonition to "strictly adhere to *standard, conservative,* and even *unimaginative* forms of investment," eerily echo the concept of market indexing? When he advises the defensive investor "to emphasize diversification more than individual selection," hasn't Benjamin Graham come within inches of describing the modern-day stock index fund?

Late in his life, in an interview published in 1976, Graham candidly acknowledged the inevitable failure of individual investment managers to outpace the market. (Again coincidentally, the interview took place at the very moment that the public offering of the world's first mutual index fund—First Index Investment Trust, now Vanguard 500 Index Fund—was taking place.) He was asked, "Can the average manager obtain better results than the Standard & Poor's Index over the years?" Graham's blunt response: "*No.*" Then he explained: "In effect that would mean that the stock market experts as a whole could beat themselves—a logical contradiction."*

Then he was asked whether investors should be content with earning the market's return. Graham's answer: "Yes." All these years later, the idea that earning your fair share of the stock market's return is the winning strategy is the central theme of this Little Book. *Only* the classic index fund can guarantee that outcome.

Finally, he was asked about the objection made against the index fund—that different investors have

---

* That is to say, there is no evidence that professional experts earn higher returns than individual amateurs, nor that any class of institutional investor (e.g., pension managers or mutual fund managers) earns more than any other class.

different requirements. Again, Graham responded bluntly: "At bottom that is only a convenient cliché or alibi to justify the mediocre record of the past. All investors want good results from their investments, and are entitled to them to the extent that they are actually obtainable. I see no reason why they should be content with results inferior to those of an indexed fund or pay standard fees for such inferior results."

"I see no reason why investors should be content with results inferior to those of an indexed fund."

The name Benjamin Graham is intimately connected, indeed almost synonymous, with "value investing" and the search for undervalued securities. But his classic book gives far more attention to the down-to-earth basics of portfolio policy—the straightforward, uncomplicated principles of diversification and rational long-term expectations, two of the overarching themes of the little book you are now reading—than to solving the sphinxlike riddle of selecting superior stocks through careful security analysis.

Graham was also well aware that the superior rewards he had reaped using his valuation principles would be difficult to achieve in the future. In that 1976 interview, he made this remarkable concession, "I am no longer an advocate of elaborate techniques of security analysis in order to find superior value opportunities. This was a rewarding activity, say, 40 years ago, but the situation has changed a great deal since then. In the old days, any well-trained security analyst could do a good professional job of selecting undervalued issues through detailed studies; *but in the light of the enormous amount of research now being carried on, I doubt whether in most cases such extensive efforts will generate sufficiently superior selections to justify their cost.*"

It is fair to say that, by Graham's demanding standards, the overwhelming majority of today's mutual funds, largely because of their high costs and speculative behavior, have failed to live up to their promise. As a result, a new type of fund—the index fund—is now gradually moving toward ascendancy. Why? Both because of what it does—providing the broadest possible diversification—and because of what it doesn't do—neither assessing high costs nor engaging in high turnover. These paraphrases of Graham's copybook maxims are an important part of his legacy to that vast majority of shareholders who, he believed, should follow the principles he outlined for the defensive investor.

———————— ∼ ————————

"To achieve satisfactory investment results is easier than most people realize."

It is Benjamin Graham's common sense, clear thinking, simplicity, and sense of financial history—along with his willingness to hold fast to the sound principles of long-term investing—that constitute his lasting legacy. He sums up his advice: "Fortunately for the typical investor, it is by no means necessary for his success that he bring the time-honored qualities . . . of courage, knowledge, judgment and experience . . . to bear upon his program—provided he limits his ambition to his capacity and confines his activities within the safe and narrow path of standard, defensive investment. To achieve satisfactory investment results is easier than most people realize; to achieve superior results is harder than it looks."

When it's so easy—in fact unbelievably simple—to capture the stock market's returns through an index fund, you don't need to take extra risks—and wasteful costs—in striving for superior results. With Benjamin Graham's long perspective, common sense, hard realism, and wise intellect, there is no doubt whatsoever in my mind that he would have applauded the index fund.

Don't Take My Word for It

While Benjamin Graham's clearly written commentary can easily be read as an endorsement of a low-cost all-stock-market index fund, don't take my word for it. Listen instead to **Warren Buffett,** his

(continued)

protégé and collaborator whose counsel and practical aid Graham acknowledged as invaluable in the final edition of *The Intelligent Investor*. In 1993, Buffett, unequivocally endorsed the index fund. In 2006, he went even further, not only reaffirming this endorsement, but personally assuring me that, decades earlier, Graham himself had endorsed index funds. Hear Mr. Buffett: "A low-cost index fund is the most sensible equity investment for the great majority of investors. My mentor, Ben Graham took this position many years ago and everything I have seen since convinces me of its truth." I can only add, after Forrest Gump, "And that's all I have to say about that."

Chapter Seventeen

"The Relentless Rules of Humble Arithmetic"

Reprise

IF THE MESSAGE IN this book comes across as confident, please understand that it is little more than common sense. Even more, please understand that my confidence in the index fund is buttressed by the conclusions of many of the smartest, most experienced, most successful investors in the United States including Warren Buffett, Charlie Munger, and Benjamin Graham, along with top academics and endowment managers—Nobel Laureates Paul Samuelson, William Sharpe, and Daniel Kahneman and Princeton's Burton Malkiel, Yale's David Swensen, Harvard's Jack Meyer, and MIT's Andrew Lo.

To these independent experts add fund industry insiders like Magellan's Peter Lynch, former Investment Company Institute Chairman Jon Fossel, Philadelphia money manager Ted Aronson, hedge fund manager Cliff Asness, fund supermarket king Charles Schwab, and analyst Mark Hulbert. Then heed the similar advice of financial journalists, from Tyler Mathisen and Jason Zweig of *Money* magazine, to the *Economist* of London and its neighbor *The Spectator*; and Jonathan Clements and Holman Jenkins, Jr., of the *Wall Street Journal*. Perhaps even more important, don't forget the convictions of intelligent investors—hundreds of corporate and government pension funds and millions of individuals, from the very wealthy to the man on the street—who have put their money where their mouth is, now investing some $5 *trillion* in index strategies.

That confidence is further buttressed by simply looking at the record, as discussed in chapter after chapter. That record confirms the superiority of indexing—by a wide margin—over the average stock fund (and the average bond fund as well) and—by an even wider margin—over the average fund investor. Further, the superiority of the index fund is based, not on the fleeting accomplishments of a tiny handful of funds (often achieved by money managers who had ceased managing the funds' portfolios years earlier), but on the permanent accomplishments of an all-market strategy where no money manager even enters the picture. Truly, the classic index fund is the only mutual fund you can hold forever.

As John Maynard Keynes warned earlier in a different context, historical returns are of no value unless we can explain the source of those returns. In this context, let me reiterate the two basic sources of the superior returns achieved by the index fund: (1) the broadest possible diversification, eliminating individual stock risk, style risk, and manager risk, with only market risk remaining; and (2) the tiniest possible costs and minimal taxes. Together, they enable the index fund to provide the gross return earned in the stock market, minus a scintilla of cost.

The two sources of the superior returns of the index fund: (1) the broadest possible diversification; and (2) the tiniest possible costs.

Actively managed equity mutual funds as a group also provide, as common sense tells you, a gross return equal to the average return of the market. Today, holding almost 25 percent of all U.S. stocks, they trade largely with one another, enriching on balance only the brokers who receive the commissions on their vigorous trading of portfolio securities (and who also happen to sell their shares) and the management companies that control them, as a result impoverishing, as it were, the net returns that the funds deliver to their investors.

Fund investment managers, distributors, marketers, administrators, brokers, and investment bankers have garnered staggering rewards for themselves. But the high prices they charge for their services, their high turnover policies and the attendant transaction costs, and the excessive taxes that their investors incur have siphoned off an enormous portion of the high real returns provided by the stock market in the past. With the subdued real returns on stocks that seem almost destined to prevail in the future (discussed in Chapter 7), those same huge rewards to those in the fund business will confiscate an even larger share—indeed, the lion's share—of the stock market's real return.

On the one hand, it is as certain as the rising and setting of the sun that the large cost advantage that exists for the index fund will continue in the years ahead. Price competition among index funds will keep the expense ratios of the low-cost providers at a minuscule level. On the other hand, marketing competition and the drive for profits among the giant financial conglomerates that hold dominion over the fund industry will create strong pressure to maintain the high fee revenues generated by their actively managed funds where, tragically, investors too often ignore the impact of the baneful fees that they pay.

It is at least theoretically possible that the fund industry will at last turn from its present competition to raise prices in order to serve the interest of fund sellers, to a new competition to cut prices and serve the interest of fund buyers. But it's impossible to imagine that the huge gap between the all-in costs of the index fund and the all-in costs of the average equity fund—a gap that has now reached some 2.5 percentage points per year—will be significantly reduced. And even if the gap were slashed by one-half—which will only happen (to use a wonderful barnyard metaphor for the inconceivable) when pigs finally whistle—the classic index fund would remain the investment of choice.

There's also no guarantee that fund investors will continue to suffer that additional loss of the 3 percentage points per year of return that they have incurred in the past through the twin penalties of market timing and fund selection. If investors, however, finally realize the error of their ways, the negative impact of their counterproductive emotions could be substantially reduced in the years ahead. At some point, after all, smart investors ought to figure out for themselves that pouring money into hot funds in hot markets, and pulling money out of those funds when they turn cool, often in cold markets, is a loser's game.

On the other hand, with the craze in trading ETFs, the gap could get even larger. Whatever the case, it seems set in stone that a substantial gap between the return earned by fund investors and the returns reported by the funds themselves will continue to exist. If you expect a substantial reversal of that trend, I would simply warn: *don't count on it.*

But above all, I'm confident about the long-term success that lies in store for sound investment in business through the classic index fund and those who invest in it, because virtually the entire case that I present is based on "the relentless rules of humble arithmetic." Lest we forget, let me again take you through these commonsense rules:

1. Over the long term, stock market returns are created by real investment returns earned by real businesses—the annual dividend yield on publicly held U.S. corporations, plus their subsequent rate of earnings growth.

2. Over the short run, illusory speculative returns, caused by the impact of the change in the amount investors are willing to pay for each dollar of corporate earnings, can increase or decrease investment returns. But in the long run, the impact of speculative return washes out.

     QED 1: In investing, the winning strategy for reaping the rewards of capitalism depends on owning businesses, not trading stocks.

3. Individual businesses come and go. Given the rapid pace of technological change we face today, along

with powerful new global competition, the failure rate of individual corporations is hardly likely to falter and may well increase.

The best protection for individual investors from the risks inherent in individual stocks is the broadest possible diversification.

QED 2: Owning businesss in the aggregate through an all-market index fund is the consummate risk-reduction strategy. (Broad economic risks to corporate earnings and dividends, however, cannot be diversified away.)

4. As a group, all investors in the stock market earn its gross returns. When the market provides an 8 percent return, investors divide up 8 percent (before taking account of costs). What else is new?

5. While investors earn the market's entire return, they do not capture the market's entire return. Rather, they capture the market's return only after the costs of financial intermediation are deducted— commissions, management fees, marketing costs, sales loads, administrative expenses, legal expenses and custodial fees, and so on. Unnecessary taxes simply enlarge the gap.

QED 3: Gross market return, minus costs, equals net return for investors as a group. (Again, remember the Gotrocks family.)

6. While all investors as a group must earn the market's net return, mutual fund investors, betrayed by their emotions (and by the fund industry) into serious errors in market timing and fund selection, have done much worse. While that gap may shrink, it is virtually inconceivable that it will be eliminated.

QED 4: Gross market return, minus costs, minus timing and selection penalties, equals the net return earned by mutual fund investors as a group.

Let me remind you again of the "4 Es" that you read about in Chapter 5: The two greatest enemies of the equity fund investor are expenses and emotions. In that context, the index fund is the investment of choice because all the other choices have serious problems. These problems begin with the grossly excessive costs that overwhelm the ability of all but the ablest (or luckiest) fund managers to outpace the index fund. But they don't end there, for the mutual fund industry has created for itself other problems that are wholly counterproductive to the interests of the investors that it seeks to serve.

———————— ∽ ————————

**Common sense suggests
that fund owners should control their funds.**

These problems include:

- The industry's very structure, in which managers control the funds that they serve under contract. Mutual funds themselves are required under the law to be governed by a board of directors that includes a majority of independent members who are unaffiliated with the management company. While common sense would suggest that the owners of the fund should be in the driver's seat of fund operations, they have been consigned to the rumble seat, essentially powerless and voiceless.

- The overriding drive among fund managers is for asset size, seemingly above all else, simply because piling assets on assets results in fees piled on fees. Yet the record shows that when small and midsize funds capitalize on their flexibility and succeed in generating exceptional returns, they draw immense cash flows and become giant funds that are muscle-bound and inflexible, limited to a return that parallels the stock market (before costs)—pinned to the earth, as it were, like Gulliver.

- The worship of the Great God Market Share, which demands aggressive and costly marketing, promotional, and advertising efforts not only to build existing funds (easiest to do with those funds that have provided superior returns in the past), but to bring out new funds with each change in the market environment. And so we had "Go-Go" funds in the 1960s; "Nifty Fifty" (proven growth stocks) funds in the 1970s; "Government-Plus" funds in the 1980s; and "New Economy" funds (notably in technology, telecommunications, or internet stocks) in the late 1990s. Today, the popular favorites include real estate funds, emerging market funds, and commodity funds. And we've added a whole new fillip: the ability to trade these funds "all day long, in real time" via the increasingly popular ETFs.

No business can forever ignore the interest of its clients. The fund industry could do so during the 1980s and 1990s only because it was blessed with the powerful tailwind of financial markets that provided the highest returns in all history—18 percent from stocks, 80 percent above the long-term average of 10 percent; 10 percent from bonds, 100 percent above the long-term average of 5 percent. But while investors seemed willing to accept the loss of a few percentage points from those enormous returns (if they were even aware of the impact of those all-in costs), they surely will not accept such a loss in the environment of sharply lower returns on stocks and bonds alike that seem certain in the years ahead. And as investors come to rely on a measurement benchmark based not on nominal returns, but on real returns, they will be even more skeptical about the ability of the fund industry to serve their interests.

**No business can forever ignore
the interest of its clients.**

The fund industry, finally, will be hoist on its own petard—an explosion created by the lethal mix of a flawed governance structure with a failed industry mission. Its unremitting aim to build enormous assets through opportunistic marketing and "new product" adventurism, all lumped on top of costs that cannot possibly be recouped by superior performance. In a brutish world peopled by smart, educated, experienced, and professional money managers who are competing with one another, managers as a group are inevitably consigned to average returns before costs; and after costs are deducted, they are destined to be losers. The arithmetic is unarguable.

"Remember, O Stranger, arithmetic is the first of the sciences." The mutual fund industry has forgotten that simple rule. Unless it changes, the industry will begin a long decline, condemned to its fate by its willingness, even its eagerness, to ignore the relentless rules of humble arithmetic. As more and more investors come to recognize the simple commonsense truth of these humble realities, the passively managed index fund is destined to become an even more formidable competitor to its actively managed rivals.

Don't Take My Word for It

Listen first to **David Swensen,** chief investment officer of Yale University, "Invest in low-turnover, passively managed index funds ... and stay away from profit-driven investment management organizations. . . The mutual fund industry is a colossal failure ... resulting from its systematic exploitation of individual investors ... as funds extract enormous sums from investors in exchange for providing a shocking disservice. . . . Excessive management fees take their toll, and (manager) profits dominate fiduciary responsibility."

Then listen to **Holman Jenkins, Jr.,** of the *Wall Street Journal,* "Will customers keep supporting the enormous overhead required to sustain ineffectual, unproductive stock picking across an array of thousands of individual funds devoted to every investing 'style' and economic sector or regional subgroup that some marketing idiot can dream up? Not likely. A brutal shakeout is coming and one of its revelations will be that stock picking is a grossly overrated piece of the puzzle, that cost control is what distinguishes a competitive firm from an uncompetitive one."

Then listen to Nobel Laureate in Economics and Princeton professor **Daniel Kahneman.** His life's work explains that investors are prone to overconfidence, and that overconfidence causes us to misinterpret information and let our emotions warp our judgment. When it comes to investing, "I don't try to be clever at all. The idea that I could see what no one else can is an illusion." So he sticks with, yes, index funds.

But for simple prose, hear this unmistakable endorsement from **Warren Buffett:** "By periodically investing in an index fund, the know-nothing investor can actually out-perform most investment professionals. Paradoxically, when 'dumb' money acknowledges its limitations, it ceases to be dumb. . . . Those index funds that are very low cost . . . are investor-friendly by definition and are the best selection for most of those who wish to own equities."

Chapter Eighteen

What Should I Do Now?

Funny Money, Serious Money, and Investment Strategy

DEEP DOWN, I REMAIN absolutely confident that the vast majority of American families will be well served by owning their equity holdings in an all-U.S. stock-market index portfolio and holding their bonds in an all-U.S. bond-market index portfolio. (Investors in high tax brackets, however, would hold a very low-cost quasi-index portfolio of high-grade intermediate-term municipal bonds.) While such an index-driven strategy may not be the best investment strategy ever devised, the number of investment strategies that are worse is infinite. The rationale for a 100-percent-index-fund portfolio remains as solid as a rock. It's all about common sense.

While an index-driven strategy may not be the best investment strategy ever devised, the number of investment strategies that are worse is infinite.

But I also fear, again deep down, that very few investors will follow that approach—the essence of simplicity—for their entire investment portfolio. You must now be as exhausted as I am by the unremitting pounding of my theme that simplicity is the answer and that complexity simply doesn't work. But we investors seem all-too-willing to ignore the verities described in this book. Instead of index funds, we opt for costly active funds and trade them to excess. Why? We are sold funds more often than we buy them. We have far too much self-confidence. We crave excitement. We succumb to the distraction that is the stock market. We fail to understand the arithmetic of investing, and the arithmetic of mutual funds.

I cannot tell you whether betting on a particular manager who pursues an active investment strategy will win or lose in the future. But I can guarantee that it hasn't worked very well in the past. To be sure, there are lots of smart, engaging, purposeful money managers and financial advisers. And all of the activity that seems endemic to the investment business can be exciting and enticing. But after all is said and done, there are no surefire solutions for investment success—wealth without risk, if you will. *It's just not a realistic expectation.* Nonetheless, building an investment portfolio can be exciting, and trying out modern remedies for age-old problems lets you exercise your animal spirits. If you crave excitement, I would encourage you to do exactly that. Life is short. If you want to enjoy the fun, enjoy! *But not with one penny more than 5 percent of your investment assets.*

That can be your Funny Money account. But at least 95 percent of your investments should be in your Serious Money account. That core of your program should consist of at least 50 percent in index funds, up to 100 percent. What about your Funny Money account? Enjoy the fun of gambling and the thrill of the chase, but not with your rent money and certainly not with college education funds for your children, nor with your retirement nest egg. Test, if you will, two or three aggressive investment strategies. You're likely to learn some valuable lessons, and it probably won't hurt you too much in the short term. Here are seven Funny Money approaches, and my advice about using them:

1. Individual stocks? *Yes.* Pick a few. Listen to the promoters. Listen to your broker or adviser. Listen to your neighbors. Heck, even listen to your brother-in-law.

2. Actively managed mutual funds? *Yes.* But only if they are run by managers who own their own firms,

who follow distinctive philosophies, and who invest for the long term, without benchmark hugging. (Don't be disappointed if the managed fund loses to the index fund in at least one year of every three!)

3. "Closet index" funds whose returns are tied closely to the returns of the stock market and that carry excessive costs? *No.*

4. Exchange traded funds? Those that track defined industry sectors that exclude the field in which the family breadwinner earns his or her living? *Maybe.* Those that hold the classic index portfolio? *Yes.* But in the Serious Money account. Whatever the case, don't speculate in ETFs. Invest in them.

5. Commodity funds? *Yes.* Of course, there will be commodity bubbles that will attract you only after they have inflated to absurd proportions. But unlike stocks and bonds, commodities have no fundamentals to support them (neither earnings and dividends nor interest payments).

6. Hedge funds? *No.* Too much hype. Too much diffusion of performance among winners and losers. Too many different strategies. Too many successful managers who won't accept your money. Too much cost and too little tax efficiency. The management fees are so high that they often destroy even the small chance you have of winning. (The hedge

fund, it is said, is not an investment strategy but a compensation strategy.)

7. Hedge funds-of-funds? *No. Really, no.* If a regular hedge fund is too expensive, just imagine a fund of hedge funds that lays on another whole layer of expenses.

**In your Serious Money Account,
50 percent to 95 percent in classic index
funds. In your Funny Money Account,
not one penny more than 5 percent.**

If you decide to have a Funny Money Account, be sure to measure your returns after one year, after five years, and after ten years. Then compare those returns with the returns you've earned in your Serious Money Account. I'm betting that your Serious Money will win in a landslide. If it does, you can then decide whether all that fun was adequate compensation for the potential wealth you've relinquished.

Fun, finally, may be a fair enough purpose for your Funny Money account. But how, you ask, should you invest your Serious Money Account—that 50 percent to 95 percent of your assets which you now depend on, or will one day depend on, for retirement? *Use an index fund strategy.* Even better, use it for 100 percent of your assets.

The fact that few of you are likely to go that far doesn't mean it isn't the best strategy. Here, listen to Warren Buffett: *"Most investors, both institutional and individual, will find that the best way to own common stocks is through an index fund that charges minimal fees. Those following this path are sure to beat the net results (after fees and expenses) delivered by the great majority of investment professionals."* (Don't forget that indexing is also, for most investors, the best way to own bonds.)

———————— ~ ————————

Reasonable alternative strategies for supplementing the index funds in your Serious Money portfolio.

While I favor the pristine and classic all-U.S.-stock-market and all-bond-market approach, there are perfectly reasonable alternative strategies for supplementing the index funds in your Serious Money portfolio. Kept within limits, here are some acceptable variations:*

- *An international flavor:* While international businesses comprise more than 30 percent of the revenues and profits of U.S. corporations, many

---

*Because of space limitations, I deal with each strategy in a cursory manner here. But further study on your part will be rewarded.

investors seek a larger global participation. Although foreign stocks account for about one-half of the world's market capitalization, I recommend that they account for no more than about 20 percent of your own equity portfolio. By far the soundest way to acquire that participation is to hold (no surprise here!) a low-cost total international index fund that tracks the returns of all non-U.S. corporations. A modest holding in a low-cost emerging market index fund is also a reasonable approach, but be sure you understand the risks.

- *Slice-and-dice:* Impressed both by the long-term performance (and recent performance) of value stocks and small-cap stocks, some investors hold the all-market (or S&P 500) index fund as the core, and add a value index fund and a small-cap index fund as satellites. I'm skeptical that any kind of superior performance will endure forever. (Nothing does!) But if you disagree, it would not be unreasonable to hold, say, 85 percent in the core, another 10 percent in value, and another 5 percent in small-cap. But doing so increases the risk that your return will fall short of the market's return, so don't push too far.

- *Bond strategy:* The all-U.S.-bond-market portfolio remains the bond investment of choice. It holds investment-grade corporate bonds, mortgage-backed

securities, and U.S. Treasurys, and has an intermediate-term maturity in the range of 5 to 10 years.
Yet we all differ in our liquidity preferences, income requirements, and tolerance for volatility.
Combining a mix of index funds linked to short-
term, intermediate-term, and long-term bonds in
varying amounts is a sound way of honoring these
preferences. I don't recommend money market
funds in this mix (they are for savings, not for investment), but rather favor short-term bond funds
for investors who lean toward greater short-term
stability of principal and in return are willing to accept less durability of income over the long term.

- *Inflation protection:* Inflation-linked bonds provide
  excellent protection against the long-term erosion
  of the purchasing power of the dollar, particularly in
  tax-deferred accounts. The U.S. Treasury offers
  these bonds in various maturities, which pays a
  basic interest rate (currently about 2.4 percent on
  the 10-year Treasury note) and is adjusted for inflation (currently expected to be about 2.3 percent).
  This all-in yield totals 4.7 percent, the same as the
  regular 10-year Treasury. The difference is that if
  inflation rises (or for that matter, falls), the total return that you earn will reflect the change. Since the
  value of Treasury note at maturity is deemed risk-

free, there is no need for the diversification of an
index fund. If you prefer a bond fund owning inflation-linked bonds, choose only the lowest-cost funds
(in effect, an index strategy).

- *Asset allocation:* How much in stocks? How much
  in bonds? Asset allocation is almost universally con-
  sidered the most important determinant of your
  long-term investment return. Most of us will want
  more stocks when we're young, have relatively small
  assets at stake, many years to recoup losses, and do
  not depend on investment income. When we're
  older, we're likely to prefer more bonds. If we've
  planned intelligently and invested wisely, our asset
  accumulations have grown to substantial size; we
  have far less time on our side; and when we have retired we will rely on our portfolios to produce a
  steady and continuing stream of income. My favorite
  rule of thumb is (roughly) to hold a bond position
  equal to your age—20 percent when you are 20, 70
  percent when you're 70, and so on—or maybe even
  your age minus 10 percent. There are no hard-and-
  fast rules here. (Most experts think my guidelines
  are too conservative. But I *am* conservative.)

- *Balanced index funds:* Since the formation of the
  first balanced index fund in 1990 (60 percent total
  U.S. stock market, 40 percent total U.S. bond

market), many variations on that theme have been created. First came *Life Strategy Funds,* each with a fixed allocation ranging from roughly 20 percent to 80 percent in stocks (often with a moderate international allocation), and the remainder in U.S. bonds. More recently, *Target Funds* have come to the fore. Here, investors can begin with an allocation appropriate to their age, which inches gradually toward a more conservative allocation as they approach the retirement age they have targeted. Such gradual rebalancing makes considerable sense. Essentially, your allocation strategy is on automatic pilot for your lifetime. The most effective way to implement this strategy is through target funds investing in stock and bond index funds. Such a strategy is likely to be carefree (even boring), just as it is likely to be enormously productive.

The low-cost index fund is especially important today in your asset allocation strategy. With the *equity premium*—the spread between the prospective stock return (about 7 percent per year) and prospective return on the U.S. 10-year Treasury Bond (now less than 5 percent)—at only about 2 percent, you can eat your cake and have it too. For index funds can deliver virtually that entire premium to investors. In contrast, even costs as low as 2 percent per year for an actively managed equity fund would erase the entire premium. Under these circumstances, for example, a fund investor with 75 percent stocks in an active equity fund and 25 percent in bonds would earn a net annual return of 5 percent per year. But an investor in a passive equity fund, pursuing a far more conservative 50/50 strategy, would earn 6 percent. *Twenty percent more return with 33 percent less risk would seem to be an offer that's too good to refuse.*

❧

For all the inevitable uncertainty amidst the eternally dense fog surrounding the world of investing, there remains much that we do know.

As you seek investment success, realize that it's never given to us to know what the returns stocks and bonds will deliver in the years ahead, nor the future returns that might be achieved by alternatives to the index portfolio. But take heart. For all the inevitable uncertainty amidst the eternally dense fog surrounding the world of investing, there remains much that we do know. Just consider these commonsense realities:

- We *know* that we must start to invest at the earliest possible moment, and continue to put money away regularly from then on.

- We know that investing entails risk. But we also know that not investing dooms us to financial failure.

- We know the sources of returns in the stock and bond markets, and that's the beginning of wisdom.

- We know that the risk of selecting specific securities, as well as the risk of selecting both managers and investment styles, can be eliminated by the total diversification offered by the classic index fund. Only market risk remains.

- We know that costs matter, overpoweringly in the long run, and we know that we must minimize them. (We also know that taxes matter, and that they, too, must be minimized.)

- We know that neither beating the market nor successfully timing the market can be generalized without self-contradiction. *What may work for the few cannot work for the many.*

- We know that alternative asset classes such as hedge funds aren't really alternative, but simply pools of capital that invest—or overinvest or disinvest—in the very stocks and bonds that comprise the portfolio of the typical investor.

- Finally, we *know* what we *don't* know. We can never be certain how our world will look tomorrow, and we know far less about how it will look a decade hence. But with intelligent asset allocation and sensible investment selections, you will be prepared for the inevitable bumps along the road and should glide right through them.

Our task remains: earning our fair share of whatever returns that our business enterprises are generous enough to provide in the years to come. That, to me, is the definition of investment success. The classic index fund is the only investment that guarantees the achievement of that goal. Don't count yourself among the losers who will fail to outpace the stock market. You will be a winner if you follow the simple commonsense guidelines in this Little Book.

Don't Take My Word for It

The ideas in this closing chapter seem like common sense to me, and perhaps they seem like common sense to you as well. But if you have any doubt, listen to their echo in these words by **Clifford S. Asness,** managing principal of AQR Capital Management. "We basically know how to invest. A good analogy is to dieting and diet books. We all know how to lose weight and get in better shape: Eat less and exercise more . . . that is *simple*—but it is not *easy.* Investing is no different. . . . Some simple, but not easy, advice for good investing and financial planning in general includes: diversify widely . . . keep costs low . . . rebalance in a disciplined fashion . . . spend less . . . save more . . . make less heroic assumptions about future returns . . . when something sounds like a free lunch, assume it is not free unless very convincing arguments are made—and then check again . . . stop watching the stock markets . . . work less on investing, not more. . . . In true Hippocratic fashion: Do No Harm! You do not need a magic bullet. Little can change the fact that current expected returns on a broad set of asset classes are low versus history. *Stick to the basics with discipline.*"

The wisdom of Cliff Asness is in fact age-old. Consider these thoughts from Benjamin Franklin, the master of common sense and simplicity. "If you would be wealthy, think of Saving as well as Getting. . . . Remember that time is money. . . . Beware of little Expenses; a small Leak will sink a great Ship. . . . There are no Gains, without Pains. . . . He that would catch Fish, must venture his Bait. . . . Great Estates may venture more, but little Boats should keep near shore. . . . Tis easy to see, hard to foresee. . . . Industry, Perseverance, and Frugality make Fortune yield."

The simple ideas in this chapter really work. A few years ago, I received this letter from a Vanguard shareholder holding our 500 Index Fund and Total Stock Market Index Fund, several of our managed equity funds and taxable and tax-exempt bond funds, and a diversified list of individual stocks.

(continued)

"Most of my shares were purchased when you were chairman. I am 85 years old and have never earned more than $25,000 a year. *I started investing in 1974 with $500. I have only bought—never sold.* I remember when things were not going well, your advice was 'stay the course.'" He enclosed a list of his investments at the start of 2004: **Total value, $1,391,407.**

As a dyed-in-the-wool indexer, of course, I believe the classic index fund must be the core of that winning strategy. But even I would never have had the temerity to say what **Dr. Paul Samuelson** of M.I.T. said in a speech to the Boston Society of Security Analysts in the autumn of 2005: *"The creation of the first index fund by John Bogle was the equivalent of the invention of the wheel and the alphabet."* Those two essentials of our existence that we take for granted every day have stood the test of time. So will the classic index fund.

Acknowledgments

IN WRITING THIS BOOK, I have received incredibly wonderful support from the entire (three-person) staff of Bogle Financial Markets Research Center, the Vanguard-supported unit that began its formal activities at the beginning of 2000.

I want to express special thanks to Assistant to the President Kevin P. Laughlin, who joined me in 1999 and is among the longest-serving of the 13 assistants who have worked with me over the years, going all the way back to 1960. Kevin has done just about everything but actually write this book—researching subjects, developing data, checking sources, helping to edit the text, working with the publisher. He has done it not only with excellence but with a patience and equanimity that have to be seen to be believed.

Emily Snyder, my executive assistant for 17 years now (and with 22 years of service on the Vanguard crew), has also been an enormous help, with extraordinary skill, steadfast finesse, and unfailing good humor. While I think she winced when I told her that, yes, I'd be writing my sixth book (and only a few short months after the publication of number five, *The Battle for the Soul of Capitalism*), she has turned my scrawled writing on piles of legal pages into a beautifully rendered typescript, and she patiently carried me through the usual eight or so edits that I can't help myself from doing—all in the pursuit of a clear, accurate, logical, and reader-friendly text.

While Sara Hoffman is new to our little group, she, too, did her share of endless typing and retyping, adjusting the rhythm of my writing to the frantic pace of our activity, also with skill, patience, and good humor.

I should note that I take full responsibility for the strong opinions expressed in this *Little Book*. These opinions do not necessarily represent the opinions of the present management of Vanguard. I remain deeply dedicated to Vanguard and its crew members, and continue to "press on, regardless" in the furtherance of the values that I invested in the firm when I founded it in 1974, and during the 25 years in which I served as chief executive, then chairman, and then senior chairman.